50 Poland Breakfast Food Recipes for Home

By: Kelly Johnson

Table of Contents

- Pierogi with cheese and potato filling
- Placki ziemniaczane (Potato pancakes)
- Kielbasa sausage with scrambled eggs
- Jajecznica (Scrambled eggs with vegetables)
- Chlodnik (Cold beet soup)
- Nalesniki (Sweet filled crepes)
- Kasza gryczana (Buckwheat groats with milk and honey)
- Babka ziemniaczana (Potato pie)
- Kopytka (Potato dumplings)
- Makowiec (Poppy seed cake)
- Zapiekanka (Open-faced sandwich with mushrooms and cheese)
- Racuchy (Yeast pancakes)
- Zurek (Sour rye soup with sausage and egg)
- Oscypek (Smoked cheese)
- Kutia (Wheat berry pudding)
- Ziemniaczki (Fried potatoes)
- Sernik (Cheesecake)
- Bundz (Sheep's milk cheese)
- Jablecznik (Apple cake)
- Kasza jaglana (Millet porridge)
- Kisiel (Fruit pudding)
- Drozdzowki (Sweet yeast buns)
- Flaki (Tripe soup)
- Zrazy (Beef rolls)
- Bialy barszcz (White borscht)
- Twarog (Farmer's cheese)
- Placki drozdzowe (Yeast pancakes)
- Zupa grzybowa (Mushroom soup)
- Pyzy (Potato dumplings)
- Krupnik (Barley soup)
- Kotlet schabowy (Breaded pork cutlet)
- Rolada (Meat roll)
- Ptasie mleczko (Chocolate-covered marshmallow)
- Zakwas (Sourdough bread)
- Zupa pomidorowa (Tomato soup)

- Bigos (Hunter's stew)
- Zrazy wolowe (Beef rolls in sauce)
- Fasolka po bretonsku (Beans with sausage)
- Tatar (Steak tartare)
- Karp smazony (Fried carp)
- Buraczki zasmazane (Fried beets)
- Mizeria (Cucumber salad)
- Krokiety (Rolled pancakes with mushrooms)
- Pani Walewska (Omelette with caviar)
- Faworki (Angel wings pastry)
- Wuzetka (Chocolate cream cake)
- Sernik na zimno (Cold cheesecake)
- Miodownik (Honey cake)
- Kremowka papieska (Papal cream cake)
- Makowiec (Poppy seed roll)

Pierogi with cheese and potato filling

Ingredients:

For the Dough:

- 2 cups all-purpose flour
- 1/2 teaspoon salt
- 1 large egg
- 1/2 cup sour cream
- 1/4 cup unsalted butter, softened
- 1/4 cup warm water (as needed)

For the Filling:

- 2 cups mashed potatoes (about 2 medium potatoes, peeled, boiled, and mashed)
- 1 cup grated farmer's cheese (or dry cottage cheese)
- 1 small onion, finely chopped and sautéed until golden brown
- Salt and pepper to taste

Instructions:

1. Make the Dough:

1. In a large bowl, combine the flour and salt.
2. In a separate bowl, whisk together the egg, sour cream, and softened butter until well combined.
3. Gradually add the wet ingredients to the flour mixture, stirring with a fork or wooden spoon until the dough starts to come together.
4. Knead the dough on a lightly floured surface until smooth and elastic, about 5-7 minutes. If the dough is too dry, add warm water, 1 tablespoon at a time, until it reaches the desired consistency.
5. Cover the dough with a damp cloth and let it rest for 30 minutes.

2. Prepare the Filling:

1. In a mixing bowl, combine the mashed potatoes, grated cheese, and sautéed onions.
2. Season with salt and pepper to taste. Mix well until everything is evenly combined.

3. Assemble the Pierogi:

1. Roll out the dough on a lightly floured surface to about 1/8 inch thickness.
2. Using a round cutter (about 3 inches in diameter), cut out circles of dough.
3. Place a small spoonful of filling in the center of each dough circle.

4. Fold the dough over the filling to create a half-moon shape. Press the edges firmly to seal, using a little water if necessary to help them stick together. You can also crimp the edges with a fork for a decorative touch.

4. Cook the Pierogi:

1. Bring a large pot of salted water to a boil.
2. Carefully drop the pierogi into the boiling water, a few at a time, stirring gently to prevent them from sticking to the bottom.
3. Cook the pierogi for about 3-5 minutes, or until they float to the surface and are cooked through.
4. Remove the cooked pierogi with a slotted spoon and drain well.

5. Serve:

1. Serve the pierogi hot, optionally topped with melted butter, sour cream, or sautéed onions.
2. Enjoy your delicious homemade pierogi with cheese and potato filling!

This recipe makes approximately 20-24 pierogi, depending on the size of your dough circles and how much filling you use for each one. Adjust the filling quantities and seasoning according to your taste preferences.

Placki ziemniaczane (Potato pancakes)

Ingredients:

- 4 medium potatoes (about 1 kg), peeled
- 1 small onion, finely grated or minced
- 2 eggs, lightly beaten
- 3 tablespoons all-purpose flour
- 1 teaspoon salt (or to taste)
- 1/2 teaspoon black pepper (or to taste)
- Vegetable oil, for frying
- Sour cream and/or applesauce, for serving (optional)

Instructions:

1. **Grate the Potatoes:**
    - Grate the peeled potatoes using a box grater or a food processor with a grating attachment. You can also use the fine shredding blade for a finer texture.
2. **Drain Excess Liquid:**
    - Place the grated potatoes in a clean kitchen towel or cheesecloth and squeeze tightly to remove excess liquid. Transfer the squeezed potatoes to a large bowl.
3. **Mix Ingredients:**
    - To the grated potatoes, add the finely grated or minced onion, beaten eggs, flour, salt, and black pepper. Mix everything together until well combined. The flour helps bind the mixture and gives the pancakes a nice texture.
4. **Fry the Pancakes:**
    - Heat a large skillet or frying pan over medium-high heat. Add enough vegetable oil to coat the bottom of the pan generously.
    - When the oil is hot (but not smoking), drop spoonfuls of the potato mixture into the pan, flattening them slightly with the back of the spoon to form pancakes about 1/4 to 1/2 inch thick.
    - Fry the pancakes for about 3-4 minutes on each side, or until they are golden brown and crispy. You may need to adjust the heat to prevent them from burning.
    - As you cook each batch, you can keep the cooked pancakes warm in a low oven (about 200°F or 95°C) on a baking sheet lined with parchment paper.
5. **Serve:**
    - Serve the potato pancakes hot, topped with sour cream and/or applesauce if desired. They are best enjoyed fresh and crispy!

Tips:

- Make sure to squeeze out as much liquid as possible from the grated potatoes to ensure crispy pancakes.
- You can adjust the seasoning to your taste preferences by adding more salt or pepper.

- For variation, you can add finely chopped fresh herbs like parsley or dill to the potato mixture before frying.

Enjoy these delicious Placki ziemniaczane as a hearty breakfast or a satisfying snack!

Kielbasa sausage with scrambled eggs

Ingredients:

- 4-6 ounces kielbasa sausage, sliced into rounds or diced
- 4 large eggs
- 1/4 cup milk or cream (optional, for creamier eggs)
- Salt and pepper, to taste
- 1 tablespoon butter or cooking oil
- Chopped fresh parsley or chives, for garnish (optional)

Instructions:

1. **Cook the Kielbasa:**
    - Heat a skillet or frying pan over medium heat. Add the sliced kielbasa sausage and cook until browned and heated through, about 3-5 minutes. Stir occasionally to ensure even cooking. If the kielbasa releases a lot of fat, you can drain some of it, but a little fat adds flavor.
2. **Prepare the Scrambled Eggs:**
    - In a bowl, whisk together the eggs and milk or cream (if using). Season with salt and pepper to taste.
    - In a separate non-stick skillet or frying pan, melt the butter or heat the cooking oil over medium heat.
    - Pour the egg mixture into the skillet and let it cook undisturbed for a few seconds until the edges begin to set.
3. **Scramble the Eggs:**
    - Using a spatula, gently push the cooked edges of the eggs towards the center of the skillet, tilting the pan to let the uncooked eggs flow to the edges. Continue cooking and gently stirring until the eggs are mostly set but still slightly creamy.
4. **Combine and Serve:**
    - Add the cooked kielbasa sausage to the scrambled eggs in the skillet. Stir gently to combine and heat through for another minute or so, ensuring the eggs are fully cooked.
    - Remove from heat and transfer the scrambled eggs and kielbasa to serving plates.
5. **Garnish and Enjoy:**
    - Garnish with chopped fresh parsley or chives if desired.
    - Serve immediately while warm, accompanied by toasted bread, rolls, or your favorite breakfast sides.

Tips:

- You can customize this dish by adding sautéed onions, bell peppers, or mushrooms along with the kielbasa.

- Adjust the seasoning to your taste preferences with additional salt, pepper, or herbs.
- Serve with crusty bread or toast for a complete breakfast experience.

This Kielbasa sausage with scrambled eggs dish is hearty, satisfying, and perfect for starting your day with a taste of Polish flavors!

Jajecznica (Scrambled eggs with vegetables)

Ingredients:

- 4 large eggs
- 1 small onion, finely chopped
- 1 small red bell pepper, diced
- 1 small zucchini, diced (optional)
- 1 medium tomato, diced
- Salt and pepper, to taste
- 2 tablespoons butter or cooking oil
- Chopped fresh herbs (such as parsley or chives) for garnish (optional)

Instructions:

1. **Prepare the Vegetables:**
    - Heat a tablespoon of butter or cooking oil in a large non-stick skillet over medium heat.
    - Add the chopped onion and sauté until translucent and slightly caramelized, about 3-4 minutes.
2. **Add the Bell Pepper and Zucchini:**
    - Add the diced red bell pepper and zucchini (if using) to the skillet. Sauté for another 3-4 minutes, until the vegetables are tender-crisp.
3. **Add the Tomato:**
    - Add the diced tomato to the skillet and cook for 1-2 minutes more, just until the tomato begins to soften.
4. **Scramble the Eggs:**
    - In a bowl, crack the eggs and whisk them together until well blended. Season with salt and pepper to taste.
    - Push the sautéed vegetables to the side of the skillet and add the remaining tablespoon of butter or oil to the empty side. Pour the beaten eggs into the skillet.
5. **Cook the Eggs:**
    - Let the eggs cook undisturbed for a few seconds until the edges start to set. Then, using a spatula, gently push the eggs from the edges towards the center of the skillet, tilting the pan to let the uncooked eggs flow to the edges.
    - Continue cooking and gently stirring until the eggs are mostly set but still slightly creamy.
6. **Combine and Serve:**
    - Once the eggs are cooked to your desired consistency, fold them into the sautéed vegetables in the skillet. Mix gently to combine everything evenly.
    - Remove from heat and transfer the scrambled eggs with vegetables to serving plates.
7. **Garnish and Enjoy:**
    - Garnish with chopped fresh herbs like parsley or chives if desired.

- Serve immediately while warm, accompanied by crusty bread, toast, or a side salad.

Tips:

- You can customize this dish by adding other vegetables such as mushrooms, spinach, or shredded carrots.
- For extra flavor, you can sprinkle grated cheese on top of the scrambled eggs just before serving.
- Adjust the seasoning according to your taste preferences with additional salt, pepper, or herbs.

This Jajecznica recipe is nutritious, filling, and packed with fresh vegetables, making it a perfect start to your day!

Chlodnik (Cold beet soup)

Ingredients:

- 3 medium beets, cooked, peeled, and grated
- 1 cucumber, peeled and diced
- 2 cups plain yogurt (or kefir)
- 1 cup sour cream
- 1-2 tablespoons lemon juice (adjust to taste)
- 2-3 tablespoons chopped fresh dill
- 1 tablespoon chopped fresh chives (optional)
- 1 tablespoon sugar (optional, to balance the acidity)
- Salt and pepper, to taste
- Hard-boiled eggs, diced (for garnish)
- Fresh dill sprigs (for garnish)
- Radishes, thinly sliced (for garnish)
- Additional cucumber slices (for garnish)

Instructions:

1. **Prepare the Beets:**
    - Wash the beets thoroughly, trim off the tops, and cook them in boiling water until tender (about 30-45 minutes, depending on size). Alternatively, you can roast them in the oven wrapped in foil at 400°F (200°C) for about 1 hour until tender. Let them cool, then peel and grate them using a box grater.
2. **Prepare the Soup Base:**
    - In a large bowl, combine the grated beets, diced cucumber, yogurt (or kefir), sour cream, lemon juice, chopped dill, and chives (if using).
    - Stir well to mix everything together. The soup should have a smooth consistency but with some texture from the grated beets and cucumber.
3. **Season the Soup:**
    - Season the soup with sugar (if using), salt, and pepper to taste. Adjust the lemon juice if you prefer a more tart flavor.
4. **Chill the Soup:**
    - Cover the bowl with plastic wrap and refrigerate the soup for at least 2 hours, or until well chilled. Chłodnik is meant to be served cold.
5. **Serve:**
    - Ladle the chilled soup into serving bowls.
    - Garnish each bowl with diced hard-boiled eggs, fresh dill sprigs, thinly sliced radishes, and additional cucumber slices.
6. **Enjoy:**
    - Serve immediately and enjoy the refreshing and tangy flavors of this traditional Polish cold beet soup!

Tips:

- Chłodnik can be made ahead of time and stored in the refrigerator for up to 2 days. The flavors often develop more after sitting for a few hours.
- Adjust the thickness of the soup by adding more yogurt or sour cream if desired.
- Some variations include adding boiled potatoes or using buttermilk instead of yogurt for a lighter version.

Chłodnik is not only delicious but also a visually stunning dish that makes a perfect starter or light meal on a hot summer day.

Nalesniki (Sweet filled crepes)

Ingredients:

For the Crepes:

- 1 cup all-purpose flour
- 2 large eggs
- 1 cup milk
- 1/4 cup water
- 2 tablespoons melted butter
- 1 tablespoon granulated sugar
- 1/4 teaspoon salt
- Butter or oil for frying

For the Filling:

- Your choice of sweet filling options such as:
    - **Sweet Cheese Filling:**
        - 1 cup farmer's cheese or dry cottage cheese
        - 1/4 cup powdered sugar (or to taste)
        - 1 teaspoon vanilla extract
        - Zest of 1 lemon (optional)
    - **Fruit Jam Filling:**
        - Your favorite fruit jam or preserves (e.g., strawberry, raspberry)
    - **Sweet Cream Cheese Filling:**
        - 1 cup cream cheese, softened
        - 1/4 cup powdered sugar (or to taste)
        - 1 teaspoon vanilla extract

Instructions:

1. Make the Crepe Batter:

1. In a large mixing bowl, whisk together the flour, sugar, and salt.
2. In a separate bowl, whisk together the eggs, milk, water, and melted butter until well combined.
3. Gradually add the wet ingredients to the dry ingredients, whisking continuously until the batter is smooth and free of lumps. Let the batter rest for about 15-20 minutes.

2. Cook the Crepes:

1. Heat a non-stick skillet or crepe pan over medium heat. Brush the pan with a little butter or oil.

2. Pour a small ladleful of batter into the pan, swirling it around to coat the bottom evenly in a thin layer.
3. Cook the crepe for about 1-2 minutes, until the edges start to lift from the pan and the bottom is lightly golden. Flip the crepe and cook for another 1 minute on the other side.
4. Transfer the cooked crepe to a plate and cover with a clean kitchen towel to keep warm. Repeat with the remaining batter, stacking the cooked crepes on top of each other.

3. Prepare the Filling:

1. Choose your desired filling option:
   - For Sweet Cheese Filling: In a bowl, mix together the farmer's cheese, powdered sugar, vanilla extract, and lemon zest until smooth.
   - For Fruit Jam Filling: Spread a thin layer of fruit jam or preserves over each crepe.
   - For Sweet Cream Cheese Filling: In a bowl, beat together the cream cheese, powdered sugar, and vanilla extract until smooth and creamy.

4. Assemble the Naleśniki:

1. Place a spoonful of the filling of your choice along one edge of each crepe.
2. Roll the crepe up gently to enclose the filling, folding in the sides as you go to create a neat cylinder shape.

5. Serve:

1. Arrange the filled crepes on serving plates.
2. Optionally, dust with powdered sugar or drizzle with melted chocolate.
3. Serve warm and enjoy these delicious Polish sweet filled crepes as a delightful dessert or treat!

Tips:

- You can experiment with various fillings such as fresh fruits, Nutella, or even savory fillings like cheese and spinach for a different twist.
- Crepes can be made ahead of time and stored stacked with parchment paper between each crepe. Reheat gently before filling.
- Be creative with presentation; arrange filled crepes on a platter and garnish with fresh fruits, whipped cream, or mint leaves for a beautiful finish.

Naleśniki are versatile and can be customized to suit your taste preferences, making them a beloved dish in Polish cuisine for any occasion.

Kasza gryczana (Buckwheat groats with milk and honey)

Ingredients:

- 1 cup buckwheat groats (kasza gryczana)
- 2 cups water
- Pinch of salt
- 2 cups milk (whole milk or your choice)
- 2-3 tablespoons honey (adjust to taste)
- Fresh fruit or nuts for garnish (optional)

Instructions:

1. **Prepare the Buckwheat Groats:**
   - Rinse the buckwheat groats under cold water until the water runs clear.
   - In a medium saucepan, bring 2 cups of water to a boil. Add a pinch of salt.
   - Stir in the rinsed buckwheat groats. Reduce the heat to low, cover the saucepan, and simmer for about 10-12 minutes, or until the groats are tender and the water is absorbed. The groats should be fluffy and slightly chewy.
2. **Cook with Milk and Honey:**
   - Once the buckwheat groats are cooked, add 2 cups of milk to the saucepan.
   - Stir in 2-3 tablespoons of honey, adjusting the amount to your desired sweetness. You can add more or less honey depending on your preference.
   - Bring the mixture to a gentle simmer over medium-low heat. Stir frequently to prevent the milk from sticking to the bottom of the pan.
3. **Serve:**
   - Once the milk is heated through and the flavors are well combined (about 5-7 minutes), remove the saucepan from the heat.
   - Taste and adjust sweetness if needed.
   - Serve the buckwheat groats with milk and honey warm, garnished with fresh fruit or nuts if desired.

Tips:

- Buckwheat groats cook relatively quickly compared to other grains, so keep an eye on them to avoid overcooking.
- You can customize this dish by adding spices such as cinnamon or cardamom for extra flavor.
- For a richer taste, you can use a combination of milk and cream.
- Leftovers can be stored in the refrigerator for a day or two. Reheat gently on the stove or in the microwave, adding a splash of milk if needed to restore creaminess.

This Buckwheat groats with milk and honey recipe offers a comforting and wholesome dish that is perfect for breakfast or as a satisfying dessert. Enjoy its nutty flavor and creamy texture!

Babka ziemniaczana (Potato pie)

Ingredients:

- 2 lbs (about 1 kg) potatoes, peeled and cut into chunks
- 1 large onion, finely chopped
- 4-5 slices of bacon or ham, diced (optional, for meat lovers)
- 4 eggs, beaten
- 1/2 cup milk or cream
- Salt and pepper, to taste
- Butter or oil, for greasing the baking dish
- Fresh parsley, chopped (optional, for garnish)

Instructions:

1. **Prepare the Potatoes:**
    - Place the peeled and chopped potatoes in a large pot of salted water. Bring to a boil and cook until tender, about 15-20 minutes. Drain well and mash the potatoes until smooth.
2. **Cook the Onion and Bacon (if using):**
    - In a skillet, cook the diced bacon or ham (if using) until crispy. Remove from the skillet and set aside. In the same skillet, sauté the chopped onion until softened and lightly golden. Remove from heat.
3. **Combine Ingredients:**
    - Preheat your oven to 350°F (175°C). Grease a baking dish (round or rectangular, about 9-10 inches in diameter) with butter or oil.
    - In a large mixing bowl, combine the mashed potatoes, beaten eggs, milk or cream, sautéed onion, and cooked bacon or ham (if using). Season with salt and pepper to taste. Mix everything together until well combined.
4. **Bake the Potato Pie:**
    - Transfer the potato mixture into the greased baking dish, spreading it out evenly.
    - Bake in the preheated oven for about 40-45 minutes, or until the top is golden brown and the pie is set.
5. **Serve:**
    - Remove from the oven and let it cool slightly before slicing.
    - Garnish with chopped fresh parsley if desired.
    - Serve warm or at room temperature, accompanied by a fresh salad or pickles.

Tips:

- You can add grated cheese into the potato mixture for extra flavor.
- If you prefer a vegetarian version, omit the bacon or ham and add more onions or other vegetables like mushrooms.
- Leftovers can be stored in the refrigerator and reheated gently in the oven or microwave.

Babka ziemniaczana is a comforting dish that showcases the heartiness of potatoes with the savory flavors of onion and bacon. It's perfect for a cozy family meal or a gathering with friends!

Get smarter responses, upload files and images, and more.

Kopytka (Potato dumplings)

Ingredients:

- 2 cups mashed potatoes (about 2 medium potatoes, peeled, boiled, and mashed)
- 1 egg
- 1 teaspoon salt
- 1/4 teaspoon ground black pepper
- 1 1/2 - 2 cups all-purpose flour (plus extra for dusting)
- Butter or oil, for frying

Instructions:

1. **Prepare the Mashed Potatoes:**
   - Peel the potatoes and cut them into chunks. Place them in a pot of salted water and boil until tender, about 15-20 minutes.
   - Drain the potatoes well and mash them thoroughly until smooth. Let them cool slightly.
2. **Make the Dough:**
   - In a large mixing bowl, combine the mashed potatoes, egg, salt, and pepper.
   - Gradually add the flour, starting with 1 1/2 cups. Mix with your hands or a wooden spoon until the dough starts to come together.
   - Add more flour as needed until the dough is soft and slightly sticky but holds its shape.
3. **Form the Dumplings:**
   - On a lightly floured surface, divide the dough into portions. Roll each portion into a rope about 1/2 inch thick.
   - Cut the ropes into pieces about 1 inch long. Optionally, you can shape each piece into small oval dumplings by rolling them gently between your palms or pressing lightly with a fork to create ridges.
4. **Cook the Kopytka:**
   - Bring a large pot of salted water to a boil.
   - Carefully drop the dumplings into the boiling water, a few at a time, stirring gently to prevent sticking. Cook until the dumplings float to the surface, about 2-3 minutes. You may need to work in batches depending on the size of your pot.
5. **Serve:**
   - Remove the cooked dumplings with a slotted spoon and transfer them to a serving dish.
   - Optionally, heat a skillet over medium heat and melt some butter or heat oil. Fry the cooked dumplings briefly until they develop a golden brown crust for added flavor and texture.
   - Serve hot as a side dish with melted butter, gravy, or your favorite sauce.

Tips:

- Ensure the mashed potatoes are well-drained and cooled slightly before mixing with the other ingredients to avoid a sticky dough.
- You can freeze uncooked kopytka on a baking sheet until firm, then transfer to a freezer bag for longer storage. Cook them directly from frozen, adding a few extra minutes to the cooking time.
- Experiment with different sauces such as mushroom sauce, tomato sauce, or simply melted butter with herbs for serving.

Kopytka are a versatile and comforting dish that pairs well with a variety of flavors, making them a beloved part of Polish cuisine. Enjoy making and savoring these delicious potato dumplings!

Makowiec (Poppy seed cake)

Ingredients:

For the Dough:

- 3 cups all-purpose flour
- 1/2 cup granulated sugar
- 1/2 teaspoon salt
- 2 1/4 teaspoons active dry yeast (1 packet)
- 1/2 cup unsalted butter, melted
- 2/3 cup warm milk (110°F / 45°C)
- 2 large eggs
- 1 teaspoon vanilla extract
- Zest of 1 lemon (optional)

For the Poppy Seed Filling:

- 1 1/2 cups ground poppy seeds
- 1 cup milk
- 1/2 cup honey (or granulated sugar)
- 1/2 cup chopped nuts (optional, such as walnuts or almonds)
- 1/4 cup raisins (optional)
- Zest of 1 lemon
- 1 tablespoon butter
- 1/2 teaspoon vanilla extract
- 1/2 teaspoon ground cinnamon
- Pinch of salt

For Assembly:

- 1 egg yolk, beaten (for egg wash)
- Powdered sugar, for dusting (optional)

Instructions:

1. Make the Dough:

1. In a small bowl, dissolve the yeast and a pinch of sugar in warm milk. Let it sit for about 5-10 minutes until foamy.
2. In a large mixing bowl, combine the flour, sugar, and salt. Make a well in the center and add the melted butter, eggs, vanilla extract, and lemon zest (if using).
3. Pour the yeast mixture into the well. Mix everything together until a soft dough forms.

4. Knead the dough on a lightly floured surface for about 8-10 minutes, or until smooth and elastic. Place the dough in a greased bowl, cover with a clean kitchen towel, and let it rise in a warm place for about 1-1.5 hours, or until doubled in size.

2. Prepare the Poppy Seed Filling:

1. In a saucepan, combine the ground poppy seeds, milk, honey (or sugar), chopped nuts (if using), raisins (if using), lemon zest, butter, vanilla extract, ground cinnamon, and a pinch of salt.
2. Cook over medium-low heat, stirring constantly, for about 10-15 minutes until the mixture thickens. Remove from heat and let it cool completely.

3. Assemble and Bake:

1. Preheat your oven to 350°F (175°C). Line a baking sheet with parchment paper.
2. Punch down the risen dough and roll it out on a lightly floured surface into a rectangle, about 12x16 inches.
3. Spread the cooled poppy seed filling evenly over the dough, leaving a small border around the edges.
4. Starting from one of the longer sides, tightly roll the dough into a log. Pinch the seams and ends to seal.
5. Carefully transfer the rolled log onto the prepared baking sheet, seam side down. Shape it into a crescent or circle.
6. Brush the top of the Makowiec with beaten egg yolk for a shiny finish.
7. Bake in the preheated oven for 35-40 minutes, or until golden brown and cooked through. If the top starts to brown too quickly, cover loosely with foil.
8. Remove from the oven and let it cool on a wire rack. Dust with powdered sugar before serving, if desired.

9. Serve:

Slice and serve the Makowiec warm or at room temperature. Enjoy this delicious Polish poppy seed cake with a cup of tea or coffee!

Tips:

- If you prefer a smoother poppy seed filling, you can process the poppy seeds in a food processor before cooking.
- Makowiec can be stored at room temperature for a few days, covered tightly with plastic wrap or stored in an airtight container.
- Feel free to customize the filling by adding more nuts, dried fruits, or adjusting the sweetness to your liking.

This Makowiec recipe captures the essence of Polish baking traditions and makes for a delightful treat for any occasion!

Zapiekanka (Open-faced sandwich with mushrooms and cheese)

Ingredients:

- 1 long baguette or French bread loaf
- 2 tablespoons butter or olive oil
- 1 onion, thinly sliced
- 2 cups mushrooms, sliced (button mushrooms or any variety you prefer)
- Salt and pepper, to taste
- 1 cup grated cheese (Gouda, mozzarella, or any melting cheese)
- Ketchup or other sauces (optional, for serving)

Instructions:

1. **Prepare the Bread:**
    - Preheat your oven to 400°F (200°C).
    - Slice the baguette or French bread loaf in half lengthwise, creating two long pieces.
2. **Sauté the Mushrooms:**
    - In a large skillet, melt the butter or heat the olive oil over medium heat.
    - Add the thinly sliced onion and sauté until softened and lightly caramelized, about 5-7 minutes.
    - Add the sliced mushrooms to the skillet. Cook, stirring occasionally, until the mushrooms are tender and any liquid released has evaporated.
    - Season with salt and pepper to taste. Remove from heat.
3. **Assemble the Zapiekanka:**
    - Place the halved baguette or French bread on a baking sheet, cut side up.
    - Spread the sautéed mushrooms and onions evenly over the bread.
4. **Add Cheese:**
    - Sprinkle the grated cheese over the mushrooms and onions, covering the bread evenly.
5. **Bake:**
    - Place the baking sheet in the preheated oven and bake for about 10-12 minutes, or until the cheese is melted and bubbly, and the bread is toasted.
6. **Serve:**
    - Remove from the oven and let it cool slightly before slicing into individual portions.
    - Optionally, drizzle with ketchup or other sauces before serving, if desired.

Tips:

- You can customize Zapiekanka by adding additional toppings such as cooked ham, bell peppers, tomatoes, or herbs.

- If you prefer a softer bread texture, you can wrap the assembled Zapiekanka in foil before baking.
- Zapiekanka is often served as a quick and satisfying meal, especially popular as street food in Poland.

Enjoy making and savoring this delicious Zapiekanka, perfect for a casual lunch or dinner!

Racuchy (Yeast pancakes)

Ingredients:

- 1 cup all-purpose flour
- 1 tablespoon granulated sugar
- 1/2 teaspoon salt
- 1 teaspoon active dry yeast
- 3/4 cup warm milk (about 110°F / 45°C)
- 1 large egg
- 1 tablespoon melted butter or vegetable oil
- 1/2 teaspoon vanilla extract
- Oil or butter, for frying
- Powdered sugar, for dusting (optional)
- Jam, honey, or maple syrup, for serving (optional)

Instructions:

1. **Activate the Yeast:**
   - In a small bowl, combine the warm milk and sugar. Sprinkle the yeast over the milk mixture and let it sit for about 5-10 minutes until frothy.
2. **Prepare the Batter:**
   - In a large mixing bowl, whisk together the flour and salt.
   - Make a well in the center and pour in the activated yeast mixture, beaten egg, melted butter or oil, and vanilla extract.
   - Stir the ingredients together until well combined and smooth. The batter will be thicker than regular pancake batter.
3. **Let the Batter Rise:**
   - Cover the bowl with a clean kitchen towel or plastic wrap and let the batter rest in a warm place for about 30-45 minutes, or until it becomes slightly bubbly and doubles in volume.
4. **Cook the Pancakes:**
   - Heat a non-stick skillet or griddle over medium heat. Lightly grease the skillet with oil or butter.
   - Spoon about 2 tablespoons of batter for each pancake onto the skillet, spreading it slightly into a round shape (racuchy are typically smaller in size compared to regular pancakes).
   - Cook the pancakes for about 2-3 minutes on each side, or until golden brown and cooked through. Adjust the heat as needed to prevent burning.
5. **Serve:**
   - Transfer the cooked racuchy to a plate and keep warm.
   - Repeat with the remaining batter, greasing the skillet between batches as needed.
   - Serve the racuchy warm, dusted with powdered sugar and optionally accompanied by jam, honey, or maple syrup.

Tips:

- Racuchy can be served plain with powdered sugar, or you can experiment with toppings such as fresh fruit, yogurt, or whipped cream.

- Ensure the skillet is adequately heated before adding the batter to achieve evenly cooked pancakes.
- Leftover racuchy can be stored in the refrigerator and reheated gently in the microwave or skillet.

Enjoy these Polish yeast pancakes, Racuchy, as a delightful and comforting breakfast or snack!

Zurek (Sour rye soup with sausage and egg)

Ingredients:

For the Soup Base:

- 1 cup fermented rye flour (żurek) or sourdough starter
- 6 cups water
- 1 onion, chopped
- 2-3 garlic cloves, minced
- 1 bay leaf
- 5-6 whole allspice berries
- 5-6 whole black peppercorns
- 1 teaspoon dried marjoram
- 1 tablespoon vegetable oil or butter
- Salt, to taste

For the Soup:

- 1/2 lb (225g) Polish sausage (kielbasa), sliced into rounds
- 2 hard-boiled eggs, peeled and sliced
- Fresh parsley, chopped (for garnish)
- Optional: sour cream or smetana, for serving

Instructions:

1. Prepare the Soup Base:

1. In a large pot, heat the vegetable oil or butter over medium heat. Add the chopped onion and sauté until translucent, about 5-7 minutes.
2. Add the minced garlic, bay leaf, allspice berries, black peppercorns, and dried marjoram to the pot. Sauté for another 1-2 minutes until fragrant.
3. In a separate bowl, mix the fermented rye flour (żurek) or sourdough starter with water until well combined and smooth.
4. Pour the rye flour mixture into the pot with the sautéed onions and spices. Stir well to combine.
5. Bring the mixture to a boil, then reduce the heat to low. Cover the pot and simmer gently for about 30-40 minutes, stirring occasionally. The soup base should thicken slightly and develop a tangy aroma.

2. Prepare the Soup:

1. Add the sliced Polish sausage (kielbasa) to the pot with the soup base. Simmer for an additional 10-15 minutes, or until the sausage is heated through and flavors meld.
2. Taste the soup and adjust seasoning with salt as needed.

3. Ladle the hot soup into bowls. Place slices of hard-boiled egg into each bowl.
4. Garnish with chopped fresh parsley.
5. Serve hot, optionally with a dollop of sour cream or smetana on top.

Tips:

- If you cannot find fermented rye flour (żurek), you can prepare a substitute by mixing equal parts rye flour and water, letting it ferment for a few days at room temperature until bubbly and sour.
- Some variations of Zurek include adding potatoes or other root vegetables for extra heartiness.
- Zurek is traditionally served in bread bowls or with a side of hearty bread.

Enjoy this comforting and flavorful Polish sour rye soup, Zurek, as a satisfying meal, especially on cooler days or as a festive dish during celebrations!

Oscypek (Smoked cheese)

Ingredients:

- 2 gallons (8 liters) whole cow's milk
- 1/4 tablet of rennet (diluted in 1/4 cup cool, non-chlorinated water)
- 1/2 teaspoon calcium chloride (if using pasteurized milk)
- 2 tablespoons cheese salt (or non-iodized salt)
- 1 cup spruce wood chips (or other suitable smoking wood chips)
- Cheesecloth
- Wooden molds (can be improvised or purchased online)

Instructions:

1. Prepare the Milk:

1. Heat the cow's milk in a large pot to 90°F (32°C). If using pasteurized milk, add calcium chloride to help with curd formation.
2. Stir in the diluted rennet thoroughly using an up-and-down motion. Cover the pot and let it sit undisturbed for 45-60 minutes, until you get a clean break when inserting a knife into the curds.

2. Cut and Cook the Curds:

1. Cut the curds into small cubes (about 1/2 inch) using a long knife. Let the curds rest for 5 minutes.
2. Slowly heat the curds to 110°F (43°C) over the course of 30 minutes, stirring gently to prevent matting.
3. Hold the curds at 110°F (43°C) for an additional 30 minutes, stirring occasionally.

3. Forming and Pressing:

1. Line the wooden molds with cheesecloth. Gently ladle the curds into the molds, pressing firmly to eliminate air pockets. Fold the cheesecloth over the top of the curds.
2. Place a follower (a piece of wood or plastic cut to fit inside the mold) on top of the curds and press at 15 lbs (7 kg) for 30 minutes.
3. Remove the cheese from the mold, unwrap it, flip it, rewrap it, and press at 25 lbs (11 kg) for 12 hours.

4. Smoking:

1. Prepare your smoker or a stovetop smoking setup. If using a stovetop method, place the wood chips in a heavy-duty foil pouch with holes punched in it to allow smoke to escape.

2. Cold smoke the cheese at around 70-80°F (21-27°C) for 4-6 hours, ensuring the temperature does not exceed 90°F (32°C). The goal is to impart a smoky flavor without melting the cheese.

5. Aging:

1. Once smoked, transfer the Oscypek to a cool, humid place (such as a refrigerator) and age it for at least 2 weeks. During this time, turn the cheese occasionally and monitor for any mold development (some molds are expected and contribute to flavor).
2. After aging, Oscypek can be stored in the refrigerator for several weeks. To serve, it is typically grilled or pan-fried until golden brown on the outside while remaining soft inside.

Tips:

- Oscypek traditionally uses sheep's milk, which provides a distinct flavor. Using cow's milk is a substitute that will give a different but still delicious result.
- Ensure all equipment and utensils are thoroughly sanitized to prevent unwanted bacteria from affecting the cheese during fermentation and aging.
- Smoking time and temperature are critical to achieve the desired smoky flavor without compromising the texture of the cheese.

Making Oscypek at home requires patience and attention to detail, but the reward is a unique and flavorful cheese that reflects Polish culinary tradition. Adjustments can be made based on equipment and ingredient availability to suit your preferences while still aiming for an authentic experience.

Kutia (Wheat berry pudding)

Ingredients:

- 1 cup wheat berries
- 4 cups water
- Pinch of salt
- 1/2 cup poppy seeds
- 1 cup hot water
- 1/2 cup honey (or more to taste)
- 1/4 cup chopped walnuts (optional)
- 1/4 cup raisins (optional)
- 1/4 cup dried apricots, chopped (optional)
- 1/4 teaspoon ground cinnamon
- 1/4 teaspoon vanilla extract
- Powdered sugar, for dusting (optional)

Instructions:

1. Prepare the Wheat Berries:

1. Rinse the wheat berries under cold water.
2. In a large pot, combine the rinsed wheat berries with 4 cups of water and a pinch of salt. Bring to a boil over medium-high heat.
3. Reduce the heat to low, cover, and simmer for about 1 to 1.5 hours, or until the wheat berries are tender and have absorbed most of the water. Stir occasionally to prevent sticking. Add more water if needed during cooking.

2. Prepare the Poppy Seeds:

1. In a small bowl, pour 1 cup of hot water over the poppy seeds. Let them soak for about 15-20 minutes.
2. Drain the poppy seeds well using a fine mesh sieve or cheesecloth.

3. Combine and Sweeten:

1. In a large mixing bowl, combine the cooked wheat berries, soaked poppy seeds, honey, chopped walnuts (if using), raisins (if using), chopped dried apricots (if using), ground cinnamon, and vanilla extract.
2. Mix everything together gently until well combined and evenly coated with honey.

4. Serve:

1. Serve Kutia either warm or cold. It's traditionally served sprinkled with powdered sugar on top.

2. Optionally, you can garnish with additional chopped nuts or dried fruits for extra texture and flavor.

Tips:

- **Make Ahead:** Kutia can be made ahead of time and stored in the refrigerator. It often tastes better the next day as the flavors meld together.
- **Variations:** Some recipes include additional ingredients like almonds, figs, or even citrus zest. Feel free to customize based on your preferences.
- **Symbolism:** Kutia is not only a delicious dessert but also a symbolic dish that represents unity, prosperity, and the hope for a bountiful year ahead.

Enjoy preparing and sharing this traditional Polish and Ukrainian dish, Kutia, with your loved ones during festive occasions!

Ziemniaczki (Fried potatoes)

Ingredients:

- 4 medium potatoes, peeled (or unpeeled, depending on preference)
- 2-3 tablespoons vegetable oil or clarified butter (ghee)
- Salt and pepper, to taste
- Optional seasonings: paprika, garlic powder, onion powder, dried herbs (such as thyme or rosemary)

Instructions:

1. **Prepare the Potatoes:**
   - Rinse and peel the potatoes (if desired) or leave the skins on for a rustic texture. Cut them into evenly sized cubes or slices, about 1/4 to 1/2 inch thick.
2. **Fry the Potatoes:**
   - Heat the vegetable oil or clarified butter (ghee) in a large skillet or frying pan over medium heat.
   - Add the potatoes to the hot oil in a single layer, ensuring they are not overcrowded. If necessary, fry them in batches.
   - Fry the potatoes, stirring occasionally, until they are golden brown and crispy on all sides. This usually takes about 10-15 minutes, depending on the size of the potato pieces and the heat of the oil.
3. **Seasoning:**
   - Once the potatoes are cooked through and crispy, season them generously with salt and pepper while they are still hot. You can also add optional seasonings like paprika, garlic powder, onion powder, or dried herbs according to your taste.
   - Toss the potatoes gently to ensure even coating of the seasonings.
4. **Serve:**
   - Transfer the fried potatoes to a serving dish lined with paper towels to absorb any excess oil.
   - Serve ziemniaczki hot as a side dish with grilled meats, chicken, fish, or as a main dish with a side of salad or vegetables.

Tips:

- **Potato Preparation:** For extra crispy ziemniaczki, you can parboil the potatoes for a few minutes before frying them. This helps to soften the inside while ensuring a crispy exterior.
- **Variations:** Feel free to customize your ziemniaczki with additional ingredients such as diced onions, bell peppers, or even bacon bits for added flavor.
- **Leftovers:** Fried potatoes can be stored in the refrigerator for a few days. Reheat them in the oven or toaster oven to maintain their crispiness.

Ziemniaczki are a comforting and versatile dish that complements many meals, offering a satisfying crunch and delightful flavor that everyone will enjoy.

Sernik (Cheesecake)

Ingredients:

For the Crust:

- 200g (about 7 oz) digestive biscuits or graham crackers, crushed
- 100g (about 7 tbsp) unsalted butter, melted

For the Filling:

- 900g (about 32 oz or 4 cups) farmer's cheese (twaróg) or dry cottage cheese
- 200g (about 1 cup) granulated sugar
- 4 large eggs, at room temperature
- 1 tbsp vanilla extract
- Zest of 1 lemon (optional)
- 1/4 cup all-purpose flour
- 200ml (about 3/4 cup) sour cream

For Serving (optional):

- Powdered sugar, for dusting
- Fresh berries or fruit compote

Instructions:

1. Prepare the Crust:

1. Preheat your oven to 350°F (175°C). Grease a 9-inch (23cm) springform pan.
2. In a mixing bowl, combine the crushed digestive biscuits or graham crackers with the melted butter until the crumbs are evenly moistened.
3. Press the mixture firmly into the bottom of the prepared springform pan to form an even crust. Set aside.

2. Make the Filling:

1. In a large mixing bowl, combine the farmer's cheese (twaróg) or dry cottage cheese with granulated sugar. Mix well until smooth and creamy.
2. Add the eggs, one at a time, mixing well after each addition.
3. Stir in the vanilla extract and lemon zest (if using).
4. Gradually add the flour, mixing until fully incorporated.
5. Finally, fold in the sour cream until smooth and well combined.

3. Assemble and Bake:

1. Pour the cheese filling over the prepared crust in the springform pan, spreading it evenly with a spatula.
2. Smooth the top with the back of a spoon.
3. Bake in the preheated oven for 50-60 minutes, or until the cheesecake is set and the top is lightly golden brown. The center should still have a slight jiggle when gently shaken.
4. Remove from the oven and let the cheesecake cool completely in the pan on a wire rack.

4. Serve:

1. Once cooled, refrigerate the cheesecake for at least 4 hours or overnight to firm up.
2. Before serving, optionally dust the top with powdered sugar.
3. Serve slices of Sernik chilled, optionally with fresh berries or fruit compote on the side.

Tips:

- **Cheese:** Traditional Polish cheesecake uses farmer's cheese (twaróg), which has a drier texture compared to cream cheese. If you cannot find farmer's cheese, you can use dry cottage cheese or a mixture of ricotta and cream cheese.
- **Variations:** Feel free to experiment with flavors by adding lemon juice or different extracts like almond or orange. Some recipes also include raisins or candied fruits in the filling.
- **Storage:** Leftover Sernik can be stored in the refrigerator for up to 3-4 days. Cover it loosely with plastic wrap or store it in an airtight container.

Enjoy making and sharing this delicious Polish cheesecake, Sernik, with family and friends for a delightful dessert or special occasion treat!

Bundz (Sheep's milk cheese)

Ingredients:

- 2 gallons (about 8 liters) fresh sheep's milk
- 1/4 tablet rennet, dissolved in 1/4 cup cool, non-chlorinated water
- Cheese salt or kosher salt

Equipment Needed:

- Large stainless steel pot
- Thermometer
- Cheesecloth
- Cheese mold or colander
- Cheese press or weights

Instructions:

1. Heat and Prepare the Milk:

1. In a large stainless steel pot, heat the fresh sheep's milk to around 90°F (32°C). Stir gently to ensure even heating.
2. Add the dissolved rennet to the warmed milk, stirring gently for about 1 minute to distribute evenly.
3. Cover the pot and let it sit undisturbed at room temperature for about 1-2 hours, or until the milk forms a clean break when a knife is inserted.

2. Cut and Cook the Curds:

1. Once the milk has set into curds and whey, cut the curds into small cubes using a long knife.
2. Slowly heat the curds and whey mixture to around 105°F (40°C), stirring gently to prevent the curds from matting together.
3. Hold the curds at this temperature for about 30 minutes, continuing to stir occasionally.

3. Form and Press the Cheese:

1. Line a cheese mold or colander with cheesecloth. Carefully ladle the curds into the mold, pressing lightly to remove excess whey.
2. Fold the cheesecloth over the top of the curds. Place a light weight on top of the cheese (about 5-10 lbs) to press it gently.
3. Let the cheese drain and continue pressing for 6-8 hours, or until it holds its shape and has reached the desired firmness.

4. Salt and Age (Optional):

1. Remove the cheese from the mold and gently sprinkle salt over the surface of the cheese.
2. If desired, you can age Bundz in a cool, humid environment (like a refrigerator) for 1-2 weeks to develop more complex flavors. Turn the cheese daily and monitor for any mold development (some molds are normal and can be wiped off).
3. Alternatively, Bundz can be enjoyed fresh without aging.

Notes:

- **Freshness:** Bundz is best enjoyed fresh, but aging can enhance its flavor and texture.
- **Storage:** Store Bundz in the refrigerator wrapped in wax paper or parchment paper. Use it within a few weeks for best quality.
- **Variations:** Experiment with different milk sources or additions like herbs or spices for flavored Bundz.

Making Bundz at home allows you to experience the traditional flavors of Polish sheep's milk cheese and enjoy it in various culinary preparations. Adjust the recipe based on your equipment and preferences to achieve the desired texture and flavor of this delicious cheese.

Jablecznik (Apple cake)

Ingredients:

For the Cake Layers:

- 2 cups all-purpose flour
- 1 teaspoon baking powder
- 1/4 teaspoon salt
- 1/2 cup unsalted butter, softened
- 1/2 cup granulated sugar
- 2 large eggs
- 1 teaspoon vanilla extract
- Zest of 1 lemon (optional)
- 1/4 cup milk

For the Apple Filling:

- 4-5 medium apples (such as Granny Smith), peeled, cored, and thinly sliced
- 1/2 cup granulated sugar
- 1 teaspoon ground cinnamon
- 1 tablespoon lemon juice
- 1 tablespoon unsalted butter

For Topping:

- 2 tablespoons granulated sugar
- 1/2 teaspoon ground cinnamon

Optional:

- Powdered sugar, for dusting

Instructions:

1. Preheat the Oven and Prepare the Cake Pan:

1. Preheat your oven to 350°F (175°C). Grease and flour a 9-inch (23cm) round cake pan or springform pan.

2. Prepare the Cake Batter:

1. In a medium bowl, whisk together the flour, baking powder, and salt. Set aside.
2. In a large mixing bowl, cream together the softened butter and sugar until light and fluffy.
3. Add the eggs, one at a time, beating well after each addition. Stir in the vanilla extract and lemon zest (if using).

4. Gradually add the flour mixture to the butter mixture, alternating with the milk, beginning and ending with the flour mixture. Mix until just combined.

3. Make the Apple Filling:

1. In a separate bowl, toss the sliced apples with sugar, ground cinnamon, and lemon juice until well coated.
2. In a large skillet or frying pan, melt the tablespoon of butter over medium heat. Add the coated apple slices and cook for about 5-7 minutes, stirring occasionally, until the apples are softened and caramelized slightly. Remove from heat and let cool slightly.

4. Assemble the Cake:

1. Spread half of the cake batter evenly into the prepared cake pan.
2. Arrange the cooked apple slices over the batter in an even layer, leaving a small border around the edge.
3. Spread the remaining cake batter over the apples, smoothing the top with a spatula.

5. Add the Topping:

1. In a small bowl, combine the granulated sugar and ground cinnamon for the topping. Sprinkle evenly over the top of the cake batter.

6. Bake the Cake:

1. Place the cake pan in the preheated oven and bake for 40-45 minutes, or until the cake is golden brown and a toothpick inserted into the center comes out clean.
2. Remove the cake from the oven and let it cool in the pan for 10 minutes. Then, transfer it to a wire rack to cool completely.

7. Serve:

1. Once cooled, dust the top of the Jablecznik with powdered sugar, if desired.
2. Slice and serve the Polish apple cake warm or at room temperature. Enjoy with a cup of tea or coffee!

Notes:

- **Variations:** You can add chopped nuts (such as walnuts or almonds) to the apple filling for added crunch and flavor.
- **Storage:** Store leftovers in an airtight container at room temperature for up to 3 days, or refrigerate for longer storage.

Jablecznik is a comforting and delicious dessert that showcases the flavors of fresh apples and warm spices. It's a favorite in Polish households during celebrations and gatherings, offering a taste of tradition and homemade goodness.

Kasza jaglana (Millet porridge)

Ingredients:

- 1 cup millet
- 2 cups water
- 2 cups milk (or substitute with water for a dairy-free version)
- Pinch of salt
- Optional toppings: honey, maple syrup, fresh fruits, nuts, seeds, cinnamon

Instructions:

1. **Rinse the Millet:** Rinse the millet under cold water in a fine-mesh sieve to remove any impurities.
2. **Toast the Millet (optional):** In a dry saucepan over medium heat, toast the rinsed millet for about 3-4 minutes, stirring frequently, until it starts to smell nutty. This step enhances the flavor of the millet, but it can be skipped if preferred.
3. **Cook the Millet:**
    - In a medium-sized saucepan, bring 2 cups of water to a boil.
    - Add the toasted or rinsed millet to the boiling water along with a pinch of salt.
    - Reduce the heat to low, cover the saucepan with a lid, and let it simmer for about 15 minutes, or until the millet absorbs most of the water and becomes tender.
    - Stir occasionally to prevent sticking and ensure even cooking.
4. **Add Milk and Simmer:**
    - Once the millet has absorbed the water, add 2 cups of milk (or water) to the saucepan.
    - Bring the mixture to a gentle simmer over medium-low heat.
    - Cook, stirring occasionally, for another 10-15 minutes or until the millet is soft and the porridge reaches your desired consistency. If the porridge becomes too thick, you can add more milk or water to adjust the consistency.
5. **Serve:**
    - Remove the saucepan from the heat.
    - Serve the kasza jaglana warm in bowls.
    - Drizzle with honey, maple syrup, or your favorite sweetener.
    - Top with fresh fruits, nuts, seeds, or a sprinkle of cinnamon for added flavor and texture.

Notes:

- **Variations:** You can customize kasza jaglana by adding flavors such as vanilla extract, almond extract, or spices like cinnamon, nutmeg, or cardamom.
- **Storage:** Leftover millet porridge can be stored in an airtight container in the refrigerator for up to 3 days. Reheat gently on the stove or in the microwave, adding a splash of milk or water to loosen the porridge as needed.

Kasza jaglana is not only delicious but also a nutritious breakfast or snack option. It's naturally gluten-free and rich in fiber, making it a wholesome addition to your diet. Enjoy this Polish millet porridge warm and topped with your favorite ingredients for a satisfying meal!

Kisiel (Fruit pudding)

Ingredients:

- 1 cup fruit juice (such as berry juice, cherry juice, or any fruit juice of your choice)
- 2 tablespoons potato starch (or cornstarch)
- 2 tablespoons sugar (adjust to taste)
- Fresh fruits (optional, for garnish)

Instructions:

1. **Mix Potato Starch with Water:**
    - In a small bowl, mix the potato starch with a little bit of cold water to create a slurry. Stir until the starch is completely dissolved.
2. **Heat Fruit Juice:**
    - In a medium saucepan, heat the fruit juice over medium heat until it starts to simmer.
3. **Add Starch Mixture:**
    - Once the fruit juice is simmering, slowly pour in the starch slurry while continuously stirring with a whisk or spoon.
4. **Cook and Thicken:**
    - Cook the mixture over medium heat, stirring constantly, until it thickens to a pudding-like consistency. This usually takes about 3-5 minutes.
5. **Sweeten:**
    - Add sugar to the pudding mixture, adjusting the amount to your taste preference. Stir well until the sugar is completely dissolved.
6. **Cool and Serve:**
    - Remove the saucepan from the heat and let the Kisiel cool slightly.
    - Pour the Kisiel into serving bowls or glasses.
7. **Chill:**
    - Refrigerate the Kisiel for at least 1-2 hours, or until it is completely chilled and set.
8. **Serve:**
    - Garnish the Kisiel with fresh fruits if desired, such as berries or slices of citrus.
    - Serve chilled as a refreshing dessert or snack.

Notes:

- **Fruit Juice:** You can use any fruit juice you like for Kisiel. Popular choices include raspberry, strawberry, cherry, or mixed berry juices. Adjust the sweetness depending on the natural sweetness of the juice.
- **Potato Starch:** Potato starch is traditionally used to thicken Kisiel, but you can substitute with cornstarch if needed.

- **Variations:** For a richer flavor, you can add a splash of lemon juice or a pinch of cinnamon to the Kisiel mixture.
- **Storage:** Store any leftover Kisiel in the refrigerator, covered, for up to 2-3 days.

Kisiel is a light and fruity dessert that is perfect for summer days or as a sweet treat after a meal. It's simple to make and can be customized with different fruits and flavors to suit your taste preferences. Enjoy this traditional Polish fruit pudding chilled for a delightful and refreshing experience!

Drozdzowki (Sweet yeast buns)

Ingredients:

For the Dough:

- 2 and 1/4 teaspoons (1 packet) active dry yeast
- 1/2 cup (120ml) warm milk (about 110°F or 45°C)
- 1/4 cup (50g) granulated sugar
- 1/2 cup (115g) unsalted butter, melted and cooled
- 2 large eggs
- 3 and 1/2 cups (440g) all-purpose flour, plus more for dusting
- 1/2 teaspoon salt

For the Filling:

- Your choice of filling: fruit jam, sweet cheese (like twaróg or farmer's cheese mixed with sugar and vanilla), poppy seed paste, or Nutella
- Optional: powdered sugar, for dusting

Instructions:

1. Activate the Yeast:

1. In a small bowl, dissolve the yeast and 1 tablespoon of the sugar in the warm milk. Let it sit for about 5-10 minutes until frothy and bubbly.

2. Make the Dough:

1. In a large mixing bowl or the bowl of a stand mixer fitted with the dough hook, combine the activated yeast mixture with the remaining sugar, melted butter, eggs, flour, and salt.
2. Mix on low speed until the dough comes together. Increase the speed to medium and knead the dough for about 5-7 minutes, or until it is smooth and elastic. If kneading by hand, knead on a floured surface for about 10 minutes.
3. Place the dough in a lightly greased bowl, cover with a clean kitchen towel or plastic wrap, and let it rise in a warm, draft-free place for about 1-2 hours, or until doubled in size.

3. Shape and Fill the Buns:

1. Punch down the risen dough to release the air.
2. Divide the dough into equal-sized portions, about the size of a golf ball (roughly 2-3 tablespoons each).
3. Flatten each portion into a circle or oval shape. Place a spoonful of your chosen filling in the center of each circle.

4. Fold the edges of the dough over the filling and pinch to seal, forming a bun shape. Place the filled buns seam-side down on a baking sheet lined with parchment paper, leaving some space between them for rising.

4. Second Rise:

1. Cover the shaped buns with a clean kitchen towel or plastic wrap and let them rise again for about 30-45 minutes, until they are puffy and have doubled in size.

5. Bake the Drożdżówki:

1. Preheat your oven to 350°F (175°C).
2. Brush the risen buns with a beaten egg wash (1 egg beaten with a tablespoon of water).
3. Bake in the preheated oven for 15-18 minutes, or until the drożdżówki are golden brown on top and cooked through.

6. Serve:

1. Remove from the oven and let the drożdżówki cool on a wire rack.
2. Optionally, dust with powdered sugar before serving.

7. Enjoy:

1. Serve drożdżówki warm or at room temperature. They are best enjoyed fresh on the day they are baked.

Notes:

- **Variations:** Feel free to experiment with different fillings such as cinnamon sugar, custard, or even savory options like cheese and ham.
- **Storage:** Store leftover drożdżówki in an airtight container at room temperature for up to 2 days. Reheat gently in the oven or microwave before serving.

Drożdżówki are a delightful treat that showcase the wonderful flavors and textures of Polish baking. Enjoy these sweet yeast buns with your favorite filling for a delicious homemade treat!

Flaki (Tripe soup)

Ingredients:

- 1 lb (450g) beef tripe, thoroughly cleaned and cut into thin strips
- 1 onion, finely chopped
- 2 carrots, peeled and diced
- 2 celery stalks, diced
- 1 parsnip, peeled and diced
- 2 cloves garlic, minced
- 1 bay leaf
- 6 cups (1.5 liters) beef broth or stock
- 1 cup (240ml) water
- 1 tablespoon tomato paste
- 1 tablespoon all-purpose flour
- 1/4 cup (60ml) white vinegar
- 1/2 cup (120ml) dry white wine (optional)
- Salt and pepper, to taste
- Chopped fresh parsley, for garnish
- Sour cream, for serving (optional)

Instructions:

1. Prepare the Tripe:

1. Thoroughly clean the beef tripe under cold water. Trim off any excess fat or tough membranes. Cut the tripe into thin strips or small squares.

2. Sauté the Vegetables:

1. In a large pot or Dutch oven, heat a bit of oil over medium heat. Add the chopped onion, carrots, celery, and parsnip. Sauté for about 5-7 minutes, until the vegetables start to soften and the onion becomes translucent.
2. Add the minced garlic and sauté for another 1-2 minutes, until fragrant.

3. Add the Tripe and Broth:

1. Add the prepared tripe to the pot with the sautéed vegetables.
2. Pour in the beef broth and water. Add the bay leaf.
3. Bring the mixture to a boil, then reduce the heat to low. Cover the pot and let it simmer gently for about 1.5 to 2 hours, or until the tripe is tender. Stir occasionally and skim off any foam that rises to the surface.

4. Thicken the Soup:

1. In a small bowl, mix the tomato paste and flour until smooth.
2. Stir the tomato paste mixture into the soup. This helps to thicken the broth slightly and adds flavor.

5. Season and Finish:

1. Add the white vinegar and dry white wine (if using) to the soup. Season with salt and pepper, to taste.
2. Continue to simmer the soup for another 15-20 minutes to allow the flavors to meld together.

6. Serve:

1. Ladle the hot Flaki into bowls. Garnish with chopped fresh parsley.
2. Serve Flaki hot, optionally with a dollop of sour cream on top.

Notes:

- **Cleaning Tripe:** Cleaning tripe thoroughly is crucial to remove any residual odor and ensure it's safe to eat. It's often soaked in water with vinegar or lemon juice before cooking to help neutralize any strong smells.
- **Variations:** Flaki can vary in ingredients and seasoning based on regional preferences in Poland. Some recipes may include additional vegetables or spices like paprika or marjoram.
- **Storage:** Flaki soup can be stored in the refrigerator for up to 3 days. Reheat gently on the stove before serving.

Flaki is a comforting and flavorful soup that showcases Polish culinary tradition. Enjoy it as a main dish or starter, especially during colder months, for a hearty and satisfying meal.

Zrazy (Beef rolls)

Ingredients:

For the Beef Rolls:

- 1.5 lbs (700g) beef round or sirloin steak, thinly sliced into 6-8 pieces
- Salt and pepper, to taste
- Dijon mustard, for spreading
- 6-8 slices bacon
- 1 large onion, finely chopped
- 1-2 dill pickles, sliced into thin strips
- 1 carrot, cut into thin strips (optional)

For the Sauce:

- 2 cups (480ml) beef broth or stock
- 1/2 cup (120ml) dry red wine
- 1 tablespoon tomato paste
- 1 tablespoon all-purpose flour
- 1 tablespoon butter
- Salt and pepper, to taste
- Chopped fresh parsley, for garnish

Instructions:

1. Prepare the Beef Rolls:

1. Place each beef slice between two sheets of plastic wrap. Use a meat mallet or rolling pin to gently pound the slices to about 1/4-inch thickness. Season each slice with salt and pepper.
2. Spread a thin layer of Dijon mustard over each beef slice.
3. Place a slice of bacon, some chopped onion, a few strips of dill pickle, and optional carrot strips on each beef slice.
4. Roll up each beef slice tightly and secure with toothpicks or kitchen twine.

2. Brown the Beef Rolls:

1. In a large skillet or Dutch oven, heat a bit of oil over medium-high heat. Add the beef rolls and sear them on all sides until browned, about 2-3 minutes per side. Work in batches if necessary to avoid overcrowding the pan.
2. Once browned, remove the beef rolls from the skillet and set them aside.

3. Make the Sauce:

1. In the same skillet, add the butter and chopped onion. Sauté until the onion becomes translucent and starts to brown, about 5-7 minutes.
2. Stir in the tomato paste and cook for another minute, stirring constantly.
3. Sprinkle the flour over the onion mixture and cook for 1-2 minutes, stirring continuously, to create a roux.
4. Gradually pour in the beef broth and red wine, stirring constantly to avoid lumps. Bring the mixture to a simmer.
5. Return the beef rolls to the skillet, nestling them into the sauce.

4. Simmer the Zrazy:

1. Cover the skillet and reduce the heat to low. Let the beef rolls simmer gently for about 1.5 to 2 hours, or until the beef is tender and cooked through, stirring occasionally.

5. Serve:

1. Remove the beef rolls from the skillet and discard the toothpicks or kitchen twine.
2. Spoon the sauce over the beef rolls and garnish with chopped fresh parsley.
3. Serve Zrazy hot, accompanied by mashed potatoes, noodles, or crusty bread.

Notes:

- **Variations:** Some variations of Zrazy may include different fillings such as mushrooms, hard-boiled eggs, or a mixture of herbs and spices.
- **Storage:** Zrazy can be stored in an airtight container in the refrigerator for up to 3 days. Reheat gently on the stove before serving.

Zrazy is a comforting and hearty dish that highlights the rich flavors of Polish cuisine. Enjoy these delicious beef rolls for a special dinner with family and friends!

Bialy barszcz (White borscht)

Ingredients:

For the Soup Base:

- 1 cup sourdough starter or 1/2 cup rye or wheat flour
- 4 cups water
- 1 onion, finely chopped
- 2 cloves garlic, minced
- 4-5 allspice berries
- 2 bay leaves
- Salt and pepper, to taste

For the Soup:

- 6 cups vegetable or chicken broth
- 1/2 lb (225g) kielbasa or Polish sausage, sliced
- 1 cup sour cream
- 2 tablespoons all-purpose flour
- 2 hard-boiled eggs, peeled and chopped
- Fresh dill, chopped, for garnish

Optional Garnishes:

- Boiled potatoes, diced
- Boiled or fried kielbasa slices
- Chopped fresh parsley

Instructions:

1. Prepare the Soup Base:

1. If using sourdough starter, combine it with 4 cups of water in a large pot. Bring to a boil, then reduce heat and simmer for 30 minutes. If using flour, mix the flour with water to form a slurry, then bring to a boil and simmer for 30 minutes.
2. Add the chopped onion, minced garlic, allspice berries, bay leaves, salt, and pepper to the pot. Simmer for an additional 10-15 minutes, until the onion is tender.

2. Prepare the Soup:

1. Strain the soup base through a fine mesh sieve or cheesecloth into a clean pot, discarding the solids.
2. Add the vegetable or chicken broth to the strained soup base and bring to a simmer over medium heat.

3. Stir in the sliced kielbasa or Polish sausage. Simmer for 10-15 minutes, until the sausage is heated through and flavors meld.

3. Thicken the Soup:

1. In a small bowl, whisk together the sour cream and flour until smooth.
2. Gradually add a ladleful of hot soup broth to the sour cream mixture, stirring constantly to temper it.
3. Pour the tempered sour cream mixture back into the pot of soup, stirring well to combine. Simmer for another 5-7 minutes, stirring occasionally, until the soup thickens slightly.

4. Serve:

1. Ladle the biały barszcz into bowls. Add diced hard-boiled eggs to each bowl.
2. Garnish with chopped fresh dill and any optional garnishes such as boiled potatoes, fried kielbasa slices, or chopped parsley.
3. Serve hot, accompanied by crusty bread or rye bread.

Notes:

- **Sourdough Starter:** Using sourdough starter adds a tangy flavor to the soup base. If you prefer a milder flavor, you can use wheat or rye flour instead.
- **Variations:** Some recipes may include additional ingredients like mushrooms, potatoes, or marjoram for added flavor.
- **Storage:** Biały barszcz can be stored in the refrigerator for up to 3 days. Reheat gently on the stove before serving, adding more broth or water if needed.

Biały barszcz is a comforting and flavorful soup that's perfect for cold days or as a special dish during holidays and celebrations. Enjoy this traditional Polish soup with its rich, creamy texture and unique sourdough or flour base!

Twarog (Farmer's cheese)

Ingredients:

- 1 gallon (4 liters) whole milk
- 1/4 cup cultured buttermilk or kefir
- Cheesecloth or muslin cloth

Instructions:

1. Heat the Milk:

1. In a large, heavy-bottomed pot, heat the whole milk over medium heat until it reaches a temperature of about 185°F (85°C), stirring occasionally to prevent scorching.
2. Once the milk reaches the desired temperature, remove it from heat.

2. Add the Culture:

1. Stir in the cultured buttermilk or kefir thoroughly into the hot milk. This will help to inoculate the milk with beneficial bacteria necessary for the fermentation process.
2. Cover the pot with a clean kitchen towel or lid and let it sit undisturbed at room temperature for 8-12 hours. During this time, the milk will thicken and curdle, forming curds and whey.

3. Strain the Curds:

1. Line a large colander or sieve with cheesecloth or muslin cloth and place it over a clean bowl or in the sink.
2. Carefully ladle or pour the curdled milk mixture into the lined colander, allowing the whey (liquid) to drain away. You can save the whey for other uses if desired.
3. Tie the corners of the cheesecloth together to create a pouch and hang it over the sink or a large bowl to drain further for 1-2 hours. The longer you drain it, the firmer the cheese will be.

4. Press the Cheese (Optional):

1. If you prefer a firmer texture, you can place the drained cheese in the cheesecloth back into the colander, place a plate or another weight on top, and refrigerate for several hours or overnight.

5. Store the Twaróg:

1. Once drained and pressed to your desired consistency, transfer the Twaróg to an airtight container and store it in the refrigerator.
2. Twaróg can be kept refrigerated for up to a week. Use it in your favorite recipes or enjoy it plain with a drizzle of honey or fresh fruit.

Notes:

- **Variations:** You can flavor Twaróg by mixing in herbs, spices, honey, or chopped fruits before serving. It's versatile and can be used in both sweet and savory dishes.
- **Usage:** Twaróg is commonly used in Polish cuisine for pierogi fillings, cheesecakes (Sernik), blintzes (Nalesniki), and as a spread on bread or toast.
- **Substitutions:** If you can't find cultured buttermilk or kefir, you can use lemon juice or white vinegar (about 1/4 cup) as a substitute to curdle the milk.

Making Twaróg at home allows you to enjoy this traditional Polish cheese in its freshest form, with the flexibility to customize its texture and flavor according to your preferences.

Placki drozdzowe (Yeast pancakes)

Ingredients:

- 1 cup (240ml) warm milk (about 110°F or 45°C)
- 1 tablespoon active dry yeast
- 1 tablespoon granulated sugar
- 2 cups (250g) all-purpose flour
- Pinch of salt
- 2 large eggs
- 1/4 cup (60ml) vegetable oil
- Butter or oil, for frying

Optional Toppings:

- Powdered sugar
- Fruit preserves or jam
- Fresh berries
- Maple syrup

Instructions:

1. Activate the Yeast:

1. In a small bowl, combine the warm milk, yeast, and sugar. Stir gently and let it sit for about 5-10 minutes until the mixture becomes frothy and bubbly.

2. Prepare the Batter:

1. In a large mixing bowl, whisk together the flour and salt.
2. Make a well in the center of the flour mixture and pour in the activated yeast mixture.
3. Add the eggs and vegetable oil to the bowl.
4. Gradually incorporate the wet ingredients into the flour mixture, stirring with a wooden spoon or a spatula, until you have a smooth batter. The batter will be thicker than traditional pancake batter but should still be pourable.
5. Cover the bowl with a clean kitchen towel or plastic wrap and let the batter rise in a warm, draft-free place for about 30-45 minutes, or until it doubles in size and becomes bubbly.

3. Cook the Pancakes:

1. Heat a non-stick skillet or griddle over medium heat. Lightly grease the skillet with butter or oil.
2. Stir the batter gently to deflate it slightly. Using a ladle or measuring cup, pour a small amount of batter onto the skillet to form pancakes of desired size (typically about 4-5 inches in diameter).

3. Cook the pancakes for 2-3 minutes on the first side, or until bubbles form on the surface and the edges start to set.
4. Flip the pancakes carefully and cook for another 1-2 minutes on the second side, until golden brown and cooked through.
5. Repeat with the remaining batter, greasing the skillet lightly as needed between batches.

4. Serve:

1. Transfer the cooked placki drożdżowe to a plate and keep warm while you cook the remaining pancakes.
2. Serve the yeast pancakes warm, topped with powdered sugar, fruit preserves, fresh berries, or maple syrup as desired.

Notes:

- **Texture:** Placki drożdżowe should be fluffy and slightly chewy due to the yeast, with a delicate sweetness from the sugar.
- **Storage:** Leftover pancakes can be stored in an airtight container in the refrigerator for up to 2 days. Reheat gently in the microwave or toaster oven before serving.

Placki drożdżowe are a wonderful treat for breakfast or brunch, offering a unique twist on traditional pancakes with their yeast-infused batter. Enjoy these Polish yeast pancakes with your favorite toppings for a delicious and satisfying meal!

Zupa grzybowa (Mushroom soup)

Ingredients:

- 1 oz (30g) dried wild mushrooms (such as porcini or mixed forest mushrooms)
- 4 cups (1 liter) vegetable or chicken broth
- 1 onion, finely chopped
- 2 cloves garlic, minced
- 1 lb (450g) fresh mushrooms (cremini, button, or wild mushrooms), cleaned and sliced
- 2 tablespoons unsalted butter or vegetable oil
- 2 tablespoons all-purpose flour
- 1 cup (240ml) sour cream
- Salt and pepper, to taste
- Fresh dill, chopped, for garnish
- Optional: 1 tablespoon soy sauce or mushroom soy sauce (for added depth of flavor)

Instructions:

1. Prepare the Dried Mushrooms:

1. Place the dried mushrooms in a bowl and cover with hot water. Let them soak for about 20-30 minutes, or until they are soft and rehydrated.
2. Drain the soaked mushrooms, reserving the soaking liquid. Chop the rehydrated mushrooms into smaller pieces if necessary.

2. Make the Soup Base:

1. In a large pot, heat the vegetable or chicken broth over medium heat until simmering.
2. Add the rehydrated mushrooms and their soaking liquid (strained through a fine sieve or cheesecloth to remove any grit) to the pot. Simmer for about 15-20 minutes to infuse the broth with mushroom flavor.

3. Sauté the Fresh Mushrooms:

1. In a separate skillet, heat the butter or vegetable oil over medium-high heat. Add the chopped onion and garlic, sautéing until softened and fragrant, about 5-7 minutes.
2. Add the sliced fresh mushrooms to the skillet and continue cooking, stirring occasionally, until the mushrooms are golden brown and any liquid they release has evaporated.

4. Thicken the Soup:

1. Sprinkle the flour over the sautéed mushrooms and stir well to coat. Cook for another 1-2 minutes, stirring constantly, to cook off the raw flour taste.
2. Gradually add a ladleful of the hot broth from the pot into the skillet, stirring constantly to create a smooth mixture (this helps to prevent lumps).
3. Pour the mushroom mixture back into the pot with the simmering broth, stirring well to combine. Simmer for another 10-15 minutes to thicken slightly.

5. Finish the Soup:

1. Reduce the heat to low. Stir in the sour cream until well incorporated. Season with salt, pepper, and optional soy sauce to taste. Adjust the consistency with additional broth or water if needed.
2. Simmer the soup gently for another 5-10 minutes to allow the flavors to meld together.

6. Serve:

1. Ladle the zupa grzybowa into bowls. Garnish with chopped fresh dill.
2. Serve the mushroom soup hot, accompanied by crusty bread or Polish rye bread.

Notes:

- **Variations:** You can vary the types of mushrooms used according to availability and preference. Some recipes include a combination of fresh and dried mushrooms for added depth of flavor.
- **Storage:** Zupa grzybowa can be stored in an airtight container in the refrigerator for up to 3 days. Reheat gently on the stove before serving, adding a splash of broth or water if needed to adjust consistency.

Zupa grzybowa is a soul-warming soup that captures the essence of Polish cuisine with its rich mushroom flavors and creamy texture. Enjoy this hearty soup as a starter or main dish during chilly days for a comforting meal.

Pyzy (Potato dumplings)

Ingredients:

For the Dough:

- 2 lbs (about 1 kg) starchy potatoes (such as russet potatoes)
- 1 cup (125g) all-purpose flour, plus more for dusting
- 1 egg
- Salt, to taste

For the Filling (Optional):

- Cooked and seasoned ground meat (e.g., pork, beef, or a mixture)
- Cooked and seasoned mushrooms
- Cheese (e.g., farmer's cheese or another melting cheese), diced

For Serving:

- Butter or oil, for frying
- Crispy bacon bits (optional)
- Sour cream
- Chopped fresh herbs (e.g., parsley or chives)

Instructions:

1. Prepare the Potatoes:

1. Peel and quarter the potatoes. Place them in a large pot of salted water and bring to a boil. Cook until the potatoes are tender when pierced with a fork, about 15-20 minutes.
2. Drain the cooked potatoes thoroughly and allow them to cool slightly.

2. Make the Dough:

1. Rice or mash the potatoes while they are still warm until smooth. Let them cool completely before proceeding.
2. In a large bowl, combine the mashed potatoes, flour, egg, and a pinch of salt. Mix until a soft dough forms. The dough should be pliable but not sticky. Add more flour if needed.

3. Form the Dumplings:

1. Divide the dough into equal portions, about the size of a small plum.
2. Flatten each portion in your hand to form a small disk. If using a filling, place a small amount (about 1 teaspoon) of the filling in the center of the disk.
3. Fold the dough over the filling to enclose it completely, shaping it into a smooth ball. Ensure the seams are sealed well to prevent the filling from leaking during cooking.
4. Repeat with the remaining dough and filling, shaping all the dumplings.

4. Cook the Pyzy:

1. Bring a large pot of salted water to a boil.

2. Carefully drop the dumplings into the boiling water. Cook in batches to avoid overcrowding, stirring gently to prevent sticking.
3. Cook the dumplings for about 5-7 minutes, or until they float to the surface. This indicates that they are cooked through.
4. Remove the cooked dumplings with a slotted spoon and transfer them to a plate.

5. Serve:

1. Heat butter or oil in a skillet over medium heat. Optionally, fry the cooked pyzy in butter or oil until golden brown and crispy on the outside.
2. Serve the pyzy hot, drizzled with melted butter or oil, and topped with crispy bacon bits (if using), sour cream, and chopped fresh herbs.

Notes:

- **Variations:** Pyzy can be served plain or filled with various ingredients like meat, mushrooms, or cheese. Experiment with different fillings to suit your taste preferences.
- **Storage:** Leftover pyzy can be stored in an airtight container in the refrigerator for up to 3 days. Reheat gently in the microwave or skillet before serving.

Pyzy are a comforting and versatile dish that showcases the heartiness of Polish cuisine. Enjoy them as a satisfying side dish or a main course, paired with your favorite toppings for a delicious meal!

Krupnik (Barley soup)

Ingredients:

- 1 cup pearl barley, rinsed

- 8 cups (2 liters) chicken or vegetable broth
- 1 onion, finely chopped
- 2 carrots, diced
- 2 celery stalks, diced
- 1 parsnip, peeled and diced (optional)
- 2 potatoes, peeled and diced
- 1 lb (450g) Polish sausage or kielbasa, sliced (optional)
- 2 tablespoons vegetable oil or butter
- 2 cloves garlic, minced
- 1 bay leaf
- 1 teaspoon dried thyme (or 1 tablespoon fresh thyme leaves)
- Salt and pepper, to taste
- Chopped fresh parsley or dill, for garnish

Instructions:

1. Prepare the Barley:

1. Rinse the pearl barley under cold water.
2. In a large pot, bring the chicken or vegetable broth to a boil. Add the rinsed barley and reduce the heat to low. Simmer for about 30 minutes, partially covered, until the barley is tender but still slightly chewy.

2. Sauté the Vegetables:

1. In a separate skillet, heat the vegetable oil or butter over medium heat. Add the chopped onion, carrots, celery, parsnip (if using), and garlic. Sauté for about 5-7 minutes, until the vegetables are softened and fragrant.

3. Add Vegetables and Sausage:

1. Add the sautéed vegetables to the pot with the cooked barley and broth.
2. Add the diced potatoes, sliced Polish sausage or kielbasa (if using), bay leaf, and dried thyme (if using dried).
3. Season with salt and pepper, to taste. Stir well to combine.

4. Simmer the Soup:

1. Bring the soup to a simmer over medium-low heat. Cover the pot and let it simmer gently for another 20-30 minutes, or until the potatoes are tender and the flavors have melded together.

5. Serve:

1. Remove the bay leaf from the soup.
2. Ladle the krupnik into bowls. Garnish with chopped fresh parsley or dill.

3. Serve hot, accompanied by crusty bread or Polish rye bread.

Notes:

- **Variations:** You can customize krupnik by adding different vegetables such as peas, cabbage, or tomatoes. Adjust the seasoning and thickness of the soup according to your preference.
- **Storage:** Krupnik soup can be stored in an airtight container in the refrigerator for up to 3 days. Reheat gently on the stove before serving.

Krupnik is a nourishing and satisfying soup that's perfect for chilly days, showcasing the wholesome flavors of barley and hearty vegetables. Enjoy this traditional Polish soup as a comforting meal for your family and friends!

Kotlet schabowy (Breaded pork cutlet)

Ingredients:

- 4 boneless pork loin chops, about 1/2-inch thick
- Salt and pepper, to taste
- 1 cup all-purpose flour
- 2 large eggs, beaten

- 1 cup fine dry breadcrumbs (preferably homemade)
- Vegetable oil, for frying
- Lemon wedges, for serving

Instructions:

1. Prepare the Pork Cutlets:

1. Place each pork loin chop between two sheets of plastic wrap or parchment paper. Use a meat mallet or rolling pin to pound the pork chops to an even thickness of about 1/4-inch.
2. Season both sides of the pork chops with salt and pepper.

2. Set Up the Breading Station:

1. Place the flour in a shallow dish or plate.
2. Beat the eggs in another shallow dish.
3. Spread the breadcrumbs in a third shallow dish.

3. Bread the Pork Cutlets:

1. Dredge each pork chop in the flour, shaking off any excess.
2. Dip the floured pork chop into the beaten eggs, ensuring it is coated evenly.
3. Press the pork chop into the breadcrumbs, covering both sides thoroughly and pressing gently to adhere.
4. Place the breaded pork cutlets on a baking sheet lined with parchment paper. Let them rest for about 10-15 minutes to allow the breading to set.

4. Fry the Kotlet Schabowy:

1. Heat vegetable oil in a large skillet over medium heat until hot but not smoking.
2. Carefully place the breaded pork cutlets in the skillet, working in batches if necessary to avoid overcrowding. Fry each cutlet for about 3-4 minutes on each side, or until golden brown and cooked through. The internal temperature of the pork should reach 145°F (63°C).
3. Transfer the fried cutlets to a plate lined with paper towels to drain excess oil.

5. Serve Kotlet Schabowy:

1. Serve the kotlet schabowy hot, garnished with lemon wedges.
2. Accompany with mashed potatoes, pickled cucumbers (ogórki kiszone), coleslaw, or your favorite side dishes.

Notes:

- **Variations:** Some recipes include a sprinkle of grated Parmesan cheese or minced herbs (such as parsley or dill) in the breadcrumb mixture for added flavor.
- **Serving Suggestions:** Kotlet schabowy pairs well with a simple salad, steamed vegetables, or Polish-style sauerkraut.
- **Leftovers:** Store any leftover kotlet schabowy in an airtight container in the refrigerator for up to 2 days. Reheat in the oven or toaster oven to maintain crispiness.

Kotlet schabowy is a classic Polish dish that's enjoyed for its crispy exterior and tender pork inside. It's a comforting meal that's sure to satisfy your taste buds!

Rolada (Meat roll)

Ingredients:

For the Meat Roll:

- 1 lb (450g) thinly sliced beef round or sirloin, about 1/4 inch thick
- 1 onion, finely chopped
- 2 cloves garlic, minced
- 1/2 cup breadcrumbs
- 1/4 cup milk
- 2 tablespoons vegetable oil
- 1 tablespoon mustard (Dijon or Polish-style)
- Salt and pepper, to taste
- 4-6 slices of bacon

For the Filling:

- 1/2 cup pickles, finely chopped
- 2 tablespoons mustard (Dijon or Polish-style)
- 1 tablespoon horseradish (optional)
- Salt and pepper, to taste

For the Gravy:

- 2 cups beef broth
- 1/4 cup all-purpose flour
- 1/4 cup sour cream
- Salt and pepper, to taste

Instructions:

1. Prepare the Meat:

1. Preheat your oven to 350°F (175°C).
2. In a bowl, soak the breadcrumbs in milk until softened.
3. In a skillet, heat the vegetable oil over medium heat. Add the chopped onion and minced garlic, and sauté until softened and fragrant, about 5 minutes. Remove from heat and let it cool slightly.
4. In a large bowl, combine the softened breadcrumbs, sautéed onions and garlic, mustard, salt, and pepper. Mix well to form a paste-like mixture.
5. Lay out the thinly sliced beef on a clean work surface. Season lightly with salt and pepper.

2. Assemble the Rolada:

1. Spread the breadcrumb mixture evenly over the beef slices, leaving a small border around the edges.
2. Sprinkle the chopped pickles over the breadcrumb mixture. Optionally, add a layer of thinly sliced bacon over the filling.

3. Starting from one end, roll up the beef slices tightly to form a log or cylinder shape. Secure the roll with kitchen twine or toothpicks at regular intervals to hold its shape.

3. Brown the Rolada:

1. In the same skillet used for onions and garlic, heat a bit more oil over medium-high heat. Carefully brown the rolled beef on all sides until golden brown, about 3-4 minutes per side.

4. Roast the Rolada:

1. Transfer the browned rolada to a roasting pan or baking dish. Optionally, add a few more slices of bacon on top.
2. Cover the roasting pan with foil or a lid and place it in the preheated oven. Roast for about 1.5 to 2 hours, or until the meat is tender and cooked through.

5. Make the Gravy:

1. Remove the rolada from the roasting pan and let it rest on a cutting board, covered with foil.
2. Place the roasting pan on the stovetop over medium heat. Add the beef broth and scrape up any browned bits from the bottom of the pan.
3. In a small bowl, whisk together the flour and sour cream until smooth. Gradually whisk this mixture into the simmering broth to thicken the gravy. Cook for a few minutes until the gravy is smooth and thickened to your liking. Season with salt and pepper, to taste.

6. Serve the Rolada:

1. Remove the kitchen twine or toothpicks from the rolada. Slice the meat roll into thick slices.
2. Serve the rolada slices hot, drizzled with the rich gravy. Optionally, garnish with fresh herbs like parsley or dill.

Notes:

- **Variations:** Some recipes for rolada may include different fillings such as hard-boiled eggs, cooked vegetables, or a combination of meats.
- **Serving Suggestions:** Rolada is traditionally served with mashed potatoes, boiled potatoes, or potato dumplings (kluski śląskie), and a side of sauerkraut or red cabbage.
- **Leftovers:** Store any leftover rolada and gravy in separate airtight containers in the refrigerator for up to 3 days. Reheat gently before serving.

Rolada is a classic Polish dish that's perfect for special occasions or family gatherings, showcasing layers of flavors and hearty textures. Enjoy this comforting meat roll with its delicious filling and savory gravy!

Ptasie mleczko (Chocolate-covered marshmallow)

Ingredients:

For the Marshmallow Filling:

- 1/2 cup (120ml) water
- 2 tablespoons unflavored gelatin
- 1 cup (200g) granulated sugar
- 1/2 cup (120ml) light corn syrup
- 1/4 teaspoon salt
- 1/2 cup (120ml) water (additional)
- 1 teaspoon vanilla extract

For the Chocolate Coating:

- 12 oz (340g) good quality semi-sweet or dark chocolate, chopped
- 2 tablespoons vegetable oil or coconut oil

Instructions:

1. Prepare the Marshmallow Filling:

1. In a small bowl, combine 1/2 cup of water with the gelatin. Let it sit and soften for about 5-10 minutes.
2. In a medium saucepan, combine the sugar, corn syrup, salt, and additional 1/2 cup of water. Stir over medium heat until the sugar dissolves.
3. Insert a candy thermometer into the saucepan and heat the mixture without stirring until it reaches 240°F (115°C) (soft ball stage).
4. Remove the saucepan from heat. Stir in the softened gelatin mixture until completely dissolved.
5. Transfer the mixture to the bowl of a stand mixer fitted with the whisk attachment (or use a hand mixer). Beat on high speed until the mixture becomes thick, white, and fluffy, about 8-10 minutes.
6. Beat in the vanilla extract until well combined.

2. Shape the Marshmallow Filling:

1. Line a baking dish or pan (about 8x8 inches) with parchment paper, leaving an overhang on the sides.
2. Pour the marshmallow mixture into the prepared pan and smooth the top with a spatula. Let it set at room temperature for at least 4 hours, or until completely firm.
3. Once set, use a sharp knife or cookie cutter to cut the marshmallow into small squares or desired shapes.

3. Coat with Chocolate:

1. Melt the chocolate and vegetable oil together in a heatproof bowl set over a pot of simmering water (double boiler method), stirring until smooth and completely melted. Alternatively, melt in the microwave in short bursts, stirring between each burst.

2. Using a fork or dipping tool, dip each marshmallow square into the melted chocolate, coating it completely.
3. Place the chocolate-covered marshmallows on a parchment-lined baking sheet. Allow any excess chocolate to drip off.
4. Let the chocolate coating set at room temperature or speed up the process by placing them in the refrigerator for about 15-20 minutes.

4. Serve or Store:

1. Once the chocolate has set, Ptasie Mleczko is ready to be enjoyed! Store them in an airtight container at room temperature for up to 1 week.

Notes:

- **Variations:** You can use different types of chocolate for coating, such as milk chocolate or white chocolate, depending on your preference.
- **Presentation:** For an authentic look, you can use a fork to create a wavy pattern on top of the chocolate coating before it sets.
- **Texture:** Ptasie Mleczko should have a soft, fluffy marshmallow center with a smooth and glossy chocolate coating.

Making Ptasie Mleczko at home allows you to enjoy this beloved Polish treat with the satisfaction of having made it yourself. It's perfect for special occasions, gifts, or simply as a delightful sweet treat!

Zakwas (Sourdough bread)

Ingredients for Zakwas (Starter):

- 100 grams rye flour (whole grain)

- 100 ml lukewarm water

Ingredients for Sourdough Bread:

- Zakwas (starter) from above
- 500 grams bread flour (all-purpose flour can also be used)
- 300 ml lukewarm water
- 10 grams salt

Instructions:

Preparing the Zakwas (Starter):

1. **Day 1:** In a clean glass jar or bowl, mix 100 grams of rye flour with 100 ml lukewarm water until well combined. Cover loosely with a cloth or plastic wrap.
2. **Day 2:** Stir the mixture well. You may notice some bubbles forming.
3. **Day 3-4:** Feed the starter by discarding half of the mixture and adding 100 grams of rye flour and 100 ml lukewarm water. Stir well. Repeat this process daily until the starter becomes bubbly and active. It may take 5-7 days, depending on ambient temperature.

Making the Sourdough Bread:

1. **Mixing the Dough:**
   - In a large mixing bowl, combine 300 ml lukewarm water with the zakwas starter.
   - Gradually add 500 grams of bread flour (or all-purpose flour) while stirring with a wooden spoon or spatula until a shaggy dough forms.
   - Cover the bowl with a damp cloth and let it rest for 30 minutes to 1 hour (autolyse).
2. **Adding Salt and Kneading:**
   - Sprinkle 10 grams of salt over the dough and knead it either in the bowl or on a lightly floured surface for about 10-15 minutes until smooth and elastic. Add a little more flour if the dough is too sticky.
   - Form the dough into a ball and place it back into the mixing bowl. Cover with a damp cloth and let it rise at room temperature for 3-4 hours, or until doubled in size. You can also place it in the refrigerator overnight for a longer fermentation.
3. **Shaping and Second Rise:**
   - After the first rise, gently deflate the dough and shape it into a loaf or place it into a well-floured proofing basket (banneton).
   - Cover with a cloth and let it rise again for 1-2 hours, until it increases in volume.
4. **Baking:**
   - Preheat your oven to 230°C (450°F). Place a baking stone or an overturned baking sheet inside to preheat.
   - Carefully transfer the risen dough onto a parchment-lined baking tray or directly onto the preheated baking stone.
   - Score the top of the loaf with a sharp knife or razor blade.

- Bake for 10 minutes at 230°C (450°F), then reduce the temperature to 200°C (400°F) and bake for another 25-30 minutes, or until the crust is deep golden brown and the bread sounds hollow when tapped on the bottom.
- Remove from the oven and let it cool on a wire rack before slicing.

Enjoy your homemade zakwas (sourdough bread) with butter, cheese, or as a delicious accompaniment to soups and stews!

Zupa pomidorowa (Tomato soup)

Ingredients:

- 1 kg ripe tomatoes, peeled and chopped (or canned tomatoes)

- 1 onion, finely chopped
- 2 cloves garlic, minced
- 2 tablespoons butter or vegetable oil
- 1 liter vegetable or chicken broth
- 2 tablespoons tomato paste
- 1 tablespoon sugar (optional, to balance acidity)
- 1 bay leaf
- 1 teaspoon dried marjoram or oregano
- Salt and pepper to taste
- Fresh basil or parsley for garnish
- Sour cream or yogurt (optional, for serving)

Instructions:

1. **Prepare the Tomatoes:**
   - If using fresh tomatoes, bring a large pot of water to a boil. Score the bottoms of the tomatoes with a small "X" and blanch them in the boiling water for about 30 seconds. Remove them with a slotted spoon and immediately transfer to a bowl of ice water to cool. Peel off the skins, chop the tomatoes, and set aside. If using canned tomatoes, skip this step.
2. **Cooking the Soup:**
   - In a large pot or Dutch oven, melt the butter (or heat the oil) over medium heat. Add the chopped onion and cook until translucent, about 5-7 minutes.
   - Add the minced garlic and cook for another minute until fragrant.
3. **Adding Tomatoes and Seasonings:**
   - Stir in the chopped tomatoes (or canned tomatoes) along with any juices. Cook for 5-7 minutes, stirring occasionally, until the tomatoes start to break down.
4. **Simmering:**
   - Pour in the vegetable or chicken broth. Add the tomato paste, sugar (if using), bay leaf, dried marjoram or oregano, salt, and pepper to taste. Stir well to combine.
   - Bring the soup to a boil, then reduce the heat to low. Cover and let it simmer gently for 20-30 minutes, stirring occasionally, until the flavors meld together and the tomatoes are very tender.
5. **Blending (Optional):**
   - For a smoother texture, you can blend the soup using an immersion blender directly in the pot. Alternatively, carefully transfer the soup in batches to a blender and blend until smooth. Be cautious with hot liquids.
6. **Adjusting Seasoning and Serving:**
   - Taste the soup and adjust seasoning if needed, adding more salt, pepper, or sugar to balance the flavors.
   - Serve hot, garnished with fresh basil or parsley leaves. Optionally, swirl in a spoonful of sour cream or yogurt for added richness.
7. **Enjoy:**

- Serve the zupa pomidorowa as a comforting starter or light main dish, accompanied by crusty bread or croutons for dipping.

This tomato soup is a delicious representation of Polish cuisine, perfect for warming up on chilly days or enjoying year-round.

Bigos (Hunter's stew)

Ingredients:

- 500 grams sauerkraut, drained and rinsed

- 500 grams fresh white cabbage, shredded
- 300 grams mixed meats (e.g., pork shoulder, beef stew meat, bacon), diced
- 200 grams Polish sausage (kielbasa), sliced
- 1 large onion, chopped
- 2 cloves garlic, minced
- 2 tablespoons tomato paste
- 1 cup dry red wine
- 1 cup beef or vegetable broth
- 2 bay leaves
- 1 teaspoon dried marjoram
- 1 teaspoon caraway seeds
- Salt and pepper to taste
- 2 tablespoons vegetable oil or butter
- Optional: dried mushrooms (porcini), soaked in hot water and chopped

Instructions:

1. **Prepare the Meats:**
   - In a large pot or Dutch oven, heat the vegetable oil or butter over medium heat. Add the diced meats (pork, beef, bacon) and sausage slices. Cook until browned on all sides, about 5-7 minutes. Remove the meats from the pot and set aside.
2. **Sauté Onion and Garlic:**
   - In the same pot, add the chopped onion and minced garlic. Cook until the onion becomes translucent, about 5 minutes.
3. **Add Sauerkraut and Cabbage:**
   - Stir in the drained sauerkraut and shredded fresh cabbage. Cook for another 5-7 minutes, stirring occasionally.
4. **Add Tomato Paste and Deglaze:**
   - Add the tomato paste to the pot and stir well to combine with the vegetables. Pour in the red wine and beef or vegetable broth, scraping the bottom of the pot to release any browned bits (this adds flavor).
5. **Season and Simmer:**
   - Return the browned meats to the pot. Add the bay leaves, dried marjoram, caraway seeds, and season with salt and pepper to taste. If using dried mushrooms, add them now as well.
   - Bring the mixture to a boil, then reduce the heat to low. Cover and let it simmer gently for at least 1.5 to 2 hours, stirring occasionally. The longer it simmers, the richer the flavors will be.
6. **Adjust Seasoning and Serve:**
   - Taste and adjust the seasoning if needed, adding more salt, pepper, marjoram, or caraway seeds as desired.
   - Bigos is traditionally served hot, accompanied by rye bread, boiled potatoes, or mashed potatoes. Some enjoy it with a dollop of sour cream on top.
7. **Storage and Reheating:**

- Bigos improves in flavor when reheated, so it's often prepared a day in advance and reheated before serving.
- Store any leftovers in the refrigerator for up to 3-4 days, or freeze for longer storage.

Bigos is a hearty and flavorful dish that reflects Polish culinary traditions, perfect for warming up during colder months or enjoying as a comforting meal year-round.

Zrazy wolowe (Beef rolls in sauce)

Ingredients:

- 4 slices of beef (round or flank steak), about 1/4 inch thick

- 4 slices of bacon
- 1 onion, finely chopped
- 2 pickles (gherkins), thinly sliced
- 1 tablespoon mustard
- Salt and pepper to taste
- Flour, for dredging
- 2 tablespoons vegetable oil
- 1 cup beef broth
- 1/2 cup dry red wine
- 2 tablespoons tomato paste
- 1 bay leaf
- 1 tablespoon all-purpose flour (optional, for thickening)
- Chopped fresh parsley, for garnish

Instructions:

1. **Prepare the beef slices:**
   - Lay out the beef slices and lightly pound them to tenderize, if needed.
   - Season each slice with salt and pepper.
2. **Prepare the filling:**
   - In a skillet, cook the bacon until crispy. Remove and drain on paper towels, then chop finely.
   - In the same skillet with the bacon fat, sauté the chopped onion until translucent. Remove from heat and let cool slightly.
   - Mix the sautéed onion with the chopped bacon and sliced pickles. Add mustard and mix well.
3. **Assemble the rolls:**
   - Place a portion of the filling on each beef slice and roll them up, securing with toothpicks or kitchen twine.
4. **Cooking:**
   - Heat the vegetable oil in a large skillet over medium-high heat.
   - Dredge each beef roll in flour, shaking off any excess.
   - Brown the rolls in the hot oil on all sides until nicely browned, about 2-3 minutes per side.
5. **Prepare the sauce:**
   - Once all rolls are browned, remove them from the skillet and set aside.
   - In the same skillet, add the beef broth, red wine, tomato paste, and bay leaf. Stir to combine and bring to a simmer.
   - Return the beef rolls to the skillet, cover, and simmer over low heat for about 1 to 1.5 hours, or until the beef is tender, stirring occasionally. Add more broth or water if needed to keep the rolls moist.
6. **Finish the dish:**

- If you prefer a thicker sauce, towards the end of cooking, mix 1 tablespoon of flour with a little water to create a slurry. Stir this into the sauce and cook for a few more minutes until thickened.
- Remove the toothpicks or twine from the beef rolls.

7. **Serve:**
    - Arrange the beef rolls on a serving platter or individual plates.
    - Spoon some of the sauce over the rolls and garnish with chopped parsley.
8. **Enjoy your Zrazy wolowe!**

Serve your Zrazy wolowe hot, accompanied by mashed potatoes or crusty bread to soak up the delicious sauce. It's a hearty and comforting dish, perfect for a satisfying meal.

Fasolka po bretonsku (Beans with sausage)

Ingredients:

- 1 lb (about 450g) dried white beans (navy beans or cannellini beans), soaked overnight
- 1 lb (about 450g) smoked sausage (kielbasa or similar), sliced into rounds
- 1 large onion, finely chopped
- 2 cloves garlic, minced
- 2 carrots, diced
- 1 celery stalk, diced
- 1 red bell pepper, diced
- 1 can (14 oz / 400g) crushed tomatoes
- 2 tablespoons tomato paste
- 1 teaspoon smoked paprika
- 1 teaspoon dried thyme (or 1 tablespoon fresh thyme leaves)
- Salt and pepper to taste
- 2 tablespoons olive oil
- Chopped fresh parsley, for garnish

Instructions:

1. **Prepare the beans:**
    - Rinse the soaked beans and place them in a large pot. Cover with water and bring to a boil. Reduce heat and simmer until beans are tender, about 1 to 1.5 hours. Drain and set aside.
2. **Cook the sausage and vegetables:**
    - In a large skillet or Dutch oven, heat the olive oil over medium heat.
    - Add the sliced sausage and cook until lightly browned, about 5-7 minutes. Remove sausage from the pan and set aside.
3. **Saute the vegetables:**
    - In the same skillet, add the chopped onion and cook until translucent, about 5 minutes.
    - Add the minced garlic, diced carrots, celery, and red bell pepper. Cook for another 5 minutes until vegetables start to soften.
4. **Combine and simmer:**
    - Stir in the crushed tomatoes, tomato paste, smoked paprika, and thyme. Season with salt and pepper to taste.
    - Add the cooked beans and browned sausage back into the skillet. Stir well to combine everything.
5. **Simmer the dish:**
    - Reduce heat to low and let the mixture simmer gently for about 30 minutes to allow the flavors to meld together. Stir occasionally to prevent sticking.
6. **Adjust seasoning and serve:**
    - Taste and adjust seasoning if needed.
    - Serve hot, garnished with chopped fresh parsley.
7. **Enjoy your Fasolka po bretonsku!**

This hearty dish is often served with crusty bread or as a side dish with grilled meats. It's comforting, filling, and perfect for a satisfying meal, especially during colder months.

Tatar (Steak tartare)

Ingredients:

- 1/2 lb (about 225g) high-quality beef tenderloin or sirloin, finely chopped or minced
- 1 small shallot, finely chopped
- 2 tablespoons capers, drained and chopped
- 2 tablespoons cornichons or pickles, finely chopped
- 1 tablespoon Dijon mustard
- 1 tablespoon Worcestershire sauce
- 1 tablespoon olive oil
- 1 tablespoon ketchup
- 1 egg yolk
- Salt and freshly ground black pepper, to taste
- Chopped fresh parsley or chives, for garnish
- Optional: Tabasco sauce or hot sauce, to taste

Instructions:

1. **Prepare the beef:**
   - Ensure the beef is very fresh and chilled. Trim any visible fat and sinew, then finely chop or mince it with a sharp knife. It's crucial to use a clean cutting board and knife for this.
2. **Mix the ingredients:**
   - In a bowl, combine the finely chopped beef with the chopped shallot, capers, cornichons, Dijon mustard, Worcestershire sauce, olive oil, and ketchup. Mix well until all ingredients are evenly distributed.
3. **Seasoning:**
   - Season the mixture with salt and freshly ground black pepper to taste. Adjust seasoning as needed. If you like it spicy, add a few dashes of Tabasco sauce or your preferred hot sauce.
4. **Serve:**
   - To serve, shape the tartare into a mound or a disc on a chilled plate using a ring mold if available.
   - Make a small indentation in the center of the tartare and carefully place the egg yolk in the hollow.
5. **Garnish:**
   - Garnish with chopped fresh parsley or chives.
6. **Accompaniments:**
   - Serve with toasted bread or baguette slices, fries, or a simple green salad.
7. **Enjoy your Tatar (Steak tartare)!**

Note: Ensure you source high-quality beef and handle it with care throughout preparation to maintain freshness and safety. Some variations of Tatar may include additional ingredients like finely chopped onion, garlic, or even anchovies for extra depth of flavor. Adjust the recipe according to your taste preferences and enjoy this classic dish as a starter or a light main course.

Karp smazony (Fried carp)

Ingredients:

- 1 whole carp (about 2-3 lbs), cleaned and scaled
- Salt and pepper, to taste
- 1 cup all-purpose flour
- Vegetable oil or clarified butter, for frying
- Lemon wedges, for serving
- Fresh parsley, chopped, for garnish (optional)

Instructions:

1. **Prepare the carp:**
    - Rinse the carp under cold water and pat dry with paper towels. Make sure the fish is scaled and cleaned properly.
2. **Seasoning and coating:**
    - Season the carp inside and out with salt and pepper.
3. **Dredge in flour:**
    - In a shallow dish or plate, spread out the flour. Dredge the carp in the flour, shaking off any excess. Ensure the fish is evenly coated.
4. **Frying:**
    - In a large skillet or frying pan, heat enough vegetable oil or clarified butter to cover the bottom of the pan over medium-high heat.
    - Carefully place the carp in the hot oil. Fry each side until golden brown and crispy, about 5-7 minutes per side depending on the size of the fish. Use tongs and a spatula to carefully flip the fish to avoid breaking it.
5. **Drain and serve:**
    - Once both sides are golden and crispy, carefully remove the carp from the skillet and place it on a plate lined with paper towels to drain excess oil.
6. **Serve:**
    - Transfer the fried carp to a serving platter. Garnish with lemon wedges and chopped fresh parsley if desired.
7. **Enjoy your Karp smażony (Fried carp)!**

This dish is traditionally served hot as a main course, accompanied by boiled potatoes or a simple salad. It's a delicious way to enjoy freshwater fish and is particularly popular in Poland during festive gatherings.

Buraczki zasmazane (Fried beets)

Ingredients:

- 4 medium-sized beets, cooked and peeled
- 1 onion, finely chopped
- 2 tablespoons butter or vegetable oil
- 1 tablespoon white vinegar or apple cider vinegar
- 1 teaspoon sugar (optional, adjust to taste)
- Salt and pepper, to taste
- Chopped fresh dill or parsley, for garnish (optional)

Instructions:

1. **Prepare the beets:**
   - Start by cooking the beets until they are tender. You can do this by boiling them in water for about 40-50 minutes or until easily pierced with a fork. Alternatively, you can roast them in the oven wrapped in foil at 400°F (200°C) for about 45-60 minutes.
2. **Cool and peel:**
   - Once the beets are cooked, let them cool slightly. Then peel off the skin using your hands or a knife (the skin should easily come off).
3. **Slice or grate the beets:**
   - Slice the cooked and peeled beets into thin rounds or grate them using a grater, depending on your preference. Sliced beets will give a bit more texture, while grated beets will cook faster and absorb flavors more readily.
4. **Fry the beets:**
   - In a large skillet or frying pan, heat the butter or vegetable oil over medium heat.
   - Add the finely chopped onion and sauté until translucent and fragrant.
5. **Add the beets:**
   - Add the sliced or grated beets to the skillet with the onions. Stir well to combine with the onions and evenly coat the beets with butter or oil.
6. **Seasoning:**
   - Season the beets with salt, pepper, and sugar (if using). The sugar helps to balance the natural sweetness of the beets and enhances their flavor.
7. **Cook and finish:**
   - Continue to cook the beets over medium heat, stirring occasionally, for about 5-7 minutes or until they are heated through and slightly caramelized.
8. **Add vinegar:**
   - Drizzle the white vinegar or apple cider vinegar over the beets and stir well to incorporate. This adds a slight tangy note to the dish.
9. **Serve:**
   - Remove the skillet from heat. Transfer the fried beets to a serving dish.
   - Garnish with chopped fresh dill or parsley if desired.
10. **Enjoy your Buraczki zasmazane (Fried beets)!**

This dish is often served warm as a side dish alongside main courses like roasted meats or poultry. It's a wonderful way to enjoy the natural sweetness and vibrant color of beets with a savory twist from frying and onions.

Mizeria (Cucumber salad)

Ingredients:

- 2 medium cucumbers
- 1/2 cup sour cream or plain yogurt
- 1-2 tablespoons fresh dill, chopped (or more to taste)
- 1/2 small red onion, thinly sliced (optional)
- 1 tablespoon white vinegar or lemon juice
- Salt and pepper, to taste
- Sugar, to taste (optional, to balance acidity)
- Chopped fresh parsley, for garnish (optional)

Instructions:

1. **Prepare the cucumbers:**
   - Peel the cucumbers if desired, or leave the skin on for extra texture. Slice the cucumbers thinly into rounds using a knife or a mandoline slicer.
2. **Salt the cucumbers:**
   - Place the sliced cucumbers in a colander and sprinkle with salt. Toss to coat evenly and let them sit for about 15-20 minutes. This helps to draw out excess moisture from the cucumbers.
3. **Prepare the dressing:**
   - In a mixing bowl, combine the sour cream or yogurt with chopped dill, white vinegar or lemon juice, and optional sugar (if using). Mix well until smooth and creamy.
4. **Assemble the salad:**
   - Pat the cucumber slices dry with paper towels to remove excess moisture. Transfer them to a serving bowl.
   - Add the sliced red onion (if using) to the cucumbers.
5. **Mix the salad:**
   - Pour the prepared dressing over the cucumbers and onions. Gently toss to coat everything evenly with the dressing.
6. **Season to taste:**
   - Taste the salad and adjust seasoning with salt and pepper as needed. You can also adjust the acidity with a bit more vinegar or lemon juice if desired.
7. **Chill and serve:**
   - Cover the salad and refrigerate for at least 30 minutes to allow the flavors to meld together.
   - Before serving, garnish with chopped fresh parsley if desired.
8. **Enjoy your Mizeria (Cucumber salad)!**

This salad is best served chilled and makes a perfect side dish for grilled meats, pierogi, or as part of a Polish meal spread. It's light, creamy, and showcases the freshness of cucumbers with a hint of dill and tanginess from the dressing.

Krokiety (Rolled pancakes with mushrooms)

Ingredients:

For the pancakes:

- 1 cup all-purpose flour
- 1 cup milk
- 1 egg
- Pinch of salt
- Butter or oil for frying

For the mushroom filling:

- 1 lb (about 450g) mushrooms, finely chopped (button mushrooms or any preferred type)
- 1 onion, finely chopped
- 2 tablespoons butter or vegetable oil
- 1 clove garlic, minced
- 1/2 teaspoon dried thyme (or use fresh thyme if available)
- Salt and pepper, to taste
- 1/2 cup sour cream or heavy cream
- 1 tablespoon all-purpose flour (optional, for thickening)

For assembly and frying:

- Butter, melted (for brushing the pancakes)
- Breadcrumbs, for coating the pancakes
- Vegetable oil or clarified butter, for frying

For the sauce (optional):

- 1 cup sour cream
- 1 tablespoon flour
- 1/2 cup chicken or vegetable broth
- Salt and pepper, to taste

Instructions:

1. **Make the pancakes:**
   - In a bowl, whisk together the flour, milk, egg, and a pinch of salt until smooth. Let the batter rest for about 15-30 minutes.
   - Heat a non-stick skillet or crepe pan over medium heat. Brush with a little butter or oil.
   - Pour a small ladleful of batter into the skillet, swirling to coat the bottom evenly. Cook for about 1-2 minutes until the edges start to lift and the bottom is lightly browned. Flip and cook the other side for another minute. Repeat with the remaining batter to make 8-10 pancakes.
   - Stack the cooked pancakes on a plate, placing parchment paper or wax paper between them to prevent sticking.
2. **Prepare the mushroom filling:**

- In a large skillet, heat butter or oil over medium heat. Add the chopped onion and sauté until softened and translucent, about 5 minutes.
- Add the minced garlic and cook for another minute until fragrant.
- Add the finely chopped mushrooms and dried thyme. Cook, stirring occasionally, until the mushrooms are tender and any liquid has evaporated, about 10-12 minutes.
- Season with salt and pepper to taste. If using, stir in the sour cream or heavy cream. If you prefer a thicker filling, mix in 1 tablespoon of flour to help thicken the mixture. Cook for another 2-3 minutes until heated through and creamy. Remove from heat and let cool slightly.

3. **Assemble and fry the krokiety:**
    - Lay out a pancake on a clean surface. Spoon a portion of the mushroom filling along one edge of the pancake.
    - Roll up the pancake tightly, tucking in the sides as you go, similar to rolling a burrito. Repeat with the remaining pancakes and filling.
    - Brush each rolled pancake (krokiet) with melted butter and roll in breadcrumbs to coat evenly.
    - In a large skillet, heat vegetable oil or clarified butter over medium heat. Fry the rolled pancakes in batches until golden brown and crispy on all sides, about 2-3 minutes per side. Drain on paper towels to remove excess oil.
4. **Make the sauce (optional):**
    - In a small saucepan, whisk together the sour cream and flour until smooth.
    - Gradually whisk in the chicken or vegetable broth until combined.
    - Cook over medium heat, stirring constantly, until the sauce thickens slightly. Season with salt and pepper to taste.
5. **Serve:**
    - Serve the krokiety hot, drizzled with the optional creamy sauce on the side.
6. **Enjoy your Krokiety (Rolled pancakes with mushrooms)!**

Krokiety are typically served as a main dish or appetizer, accompanied by a salad or pickles. They are flavorful and hearty, making them a favorite in Polish cuisine, especially during celebrations and holidays.

Pani Walewska (Omelette with caviar)

Ingredients:

- 4 large eggs

- 2 tablespoons milk or heavy cream
- Salt and pepper, to taste
- 2 tablespoons butter
- 2-3 tablespoons caviar (preferably salmon or sturgeon caviar)
- Fresh chives or parsley, chopped, for garnish (optional)
- Lemon wedges, for serving

Instructions:

1. **Prepare the eggs:**
   - Crack the eggs into a bowl. Add the milk or heavy cream, salt, and pepper. Whisk vigorously until the mixture is well combined and slightly frothy.
2. **Cook the omelette:**
   - In a non-stick skillet, melt 1 tablespoon of butter over medium heat until foamy and hot.
   - Pour the egg mixture into the skillet. Allow the eggs to set slightly around the edges, then gently push them towards the center with a spatula, tilting the skillet to let the uncooked eggs flow to the edges.
   - Continue cooking for a few more minutes until the omelette is almost set but still slightly runny on top.
3. **Add the caviar:**
   - Spoon the caviar evenly over one half of the omelette.
4. **Fold and serve:**
   - Carefully fold the omelette in half over the caviar using a spatula.
   - Slide the omelette onto a plate and garnish with chopped fresh chives or parsley if desired.
5. **Serve:**
   - Serve the Pani Walewska immediately, accompanied by lemon wedges on the side.
6. **Enjoy your Pani Walewska (Omelette with caviar)!**

This dish is a delightful combination of fluffy eggs and the rich, briny flavor of caviar. It's perfect for a special breakfast or brunch, or as an elegant appetizer for a celebratory meal. The simplicity of the ingredients allows the flavors to shine, making it a true indulgence inspired by Polish culinary tradition.

Faworki (Angel wings pastry)

Ingredients:

- 2 cups (250g) all-purpose flour

- 2 tablespoons granulated sugar
- 2 large eggs
- 2 tablespoons sour cream or plain yogurt
- 2 tablespoons unsalted butter, melted and cooled
- 1 tablespoon vodka or rum (optional, helps to make the dough crispy)
- Pinch of salt
- Vegetable oil, for frying
- Powdered sugar, for dusting

Instructions:

1. **Prepare the dough:**
   - In a large mixing bowl, combine the flour, sugar, and salt.
   - Make a well in the center and add the eggs, sour cream or yogurt, melted butter, and vodka or rum (if using).
   - Mix the ingredients together until a smooth dough forms. You can knead the dough briefly until it comes together, but avoid over-kneading.
2. **Rest the dough:**
   - Wrap the dough in plastic wrap and let it rest at room temperature for about 30 minutes.
3. **Roll out the dough:**
   - Divide the dough into smaller portions for easier handling. Roll out each portion on a lightly floured surface until very thin (about 1-2 mm thick).
   - Using a pastry cutter or a sharp knife, cut the dough into strips about 1 inch wide and 4-5 inches long. You can also make diamond shapes by cutting slits in the center of each strip.
4. **Shape the faworki:**
   - Make a small slit in the center of each strip, then pull one end through the slit to form a twisted shape resembling a bow or knot. Repeat with the remaining strips.
5. **Fry the faworki:**
   - In a large skillet or pot, heat vegetable oil over medium heat until it reaches about 350°F (175°C).
   - Fry the faworki in batches, a few at a time, until golden brown and crispy, about 1-2 minutes per side. Use tongs or a slotted spoon to turn them halfway through cooking.
6. **Drain and dust:**
   - Remove the fried faworki with a slotted spoon and drain on paper towels to absorb excess oil.
   - Dust the warm faworki generously with powdered sugar while they are still slightly warm.
7. **Serve:**
   - Arrange the faworki on a serving platter and serve them fresh and crispy.
8. **Enjoy your Faworki (Angel wings pastry)!**

These delicate pastries are best enjoyed freshly made. They are light, crispy, and perfect with a cup of tea or coffee. Faworki are a wonderful treat to celebrate Polish traditions and add a festive touch to any occasion.

Wuzetka (Chocolate cream cake)

Ingredients:

For the chocolate sponge cake:

- 4 large eggs
- 3/4 cup (150g) granulated sugar
- 1/2 cup (60g) all-purpose flour
- 1/4 cup (30g) unsweetened cocoa powder
- 1 teaspoon baking powder
- Pinch of salt

For the chocolate cream filling:

- 1 cup (240ml) heavy cream
- 8 oz (225g) dark chocolate, finely chopped
- 1 tablespoon unsalted butter

For the chocolate ganache:

- 1/2 cup (120ml) heavy cream
- 6 oz (170g) dark chocolate, finely chopped

Optional garnish:

- Chocolate curls or sprinkles

Instructions:

1. **Make the chocolate sponge cake:**
    - Preheat your oven to 350°F (180°C). Grease and line an 8-inch (20cm) round cake pan with parchment paper.
    - In a mixing bowl, whisk together the eggs and sugar until pale and fluffy.
    - In a separate bowl, sift together the flour, cocoa powder, baking powder, and salt.
    - Gradually fold the dry ingredients into the egg mixture until well combined.
    - Pour the batter into the prepared cake pan and smooth the top.
    - Bake in the preheated oven for about 25-30 minutes, or until a toothpick inserted into the center comes out clean.
    - Remove from the oven and let the cake cool in the pan for 10 minutes before transferring it to a wire rack to cool completely.
2. **Make the chocolate cream filling:**
    - In a small saucepan, heat the heavy cream over medium heat until it just begins to simmer (do not boil).
    - Remove from heat and stir in the finely chopped dark chocolate until smooth and melted.
    - Add the butter and stir until incorporated and the mixture is glossy.
    - Transfer the chocolate cream filling to a bowl and let it cool to room temperature, then refrigerate until it thickens and is spreadable.
3. **Assemble the cake:**
    - Once the cake is completely cooled, slice it horizontally into two even layers.

- Place one layer of the cake on a serving plate or cake stand. Spread a generous layer of the chocolate cream filling evenly over the cake layer.
- Place the second cake layer on top and press gently to sandwich the layers together.
4. **Make the chocolate ganache:**
    - In a small saucepan, heat the heavy cream over medium heat until it just begins to simmer.
    - Remove from heat and add the finely chopped dark chocolate. Let it sit for 1-2 minutes, then stir gently until smooth and shiny.
5. **Finish the cake:**
    - Pour the chocolate ganache over the top of the cake, allowing it to drip down the sides.
    - Use an offset spatula to spread the ganache evenly over the top and sides of the cake.
6. **Optional garnish:**
    - If desired, decorate the cake with chocolate curls or sprinkles while the ganache is still soft.
7. **Chill and serve:**
    - Refrigerate the cake for at least 1-2 hours to allow the ganache to set and the flavors to meld.
8. **Enjoy your Wuzetka (Chocolate cream cake)!**

This decadent Polish dessert is sure to impress with its rich chocolate flavor and creamy texture. It's perfect for special occasions or whenever you crave a luxurious chocolate treat.

Sernik na zimno (Cold cheesecake)

Ingredients:

For the crust:

- 200g digestive biscuits or graham crackers

- 100g unsalted butter, melted

For the cheesecake filling:

- 500g (about 2 cups) twaróg (Polish curd cheese) or farmer's cheese, strained
- 400g (about 1 3/4 cups) cream cheese, at room temperature
- 200g (about 1 cup) powdered sugar
- Zest and juice of 1 lemon
- 1 teaspoon vanilla extract
- 250ml (about 1 cup) heavy cream, whipped to stiff peaks

For garnish (optional):

- Fresh berries, fruit compote, or fruit preserves

Instructions:

1. **Prepare the crust:**
    - Crush the digestive biscuits or graham crackers into fine crumbs. You can do this in a food processor or place them in a zip-top bag and crush them with a rolling pin.
    - Transfer the crumbs to a bowl and mix in the melted butter until well combined and the mixture resembles wet sand.
    - Press the mixture evenly into the bottom of a 9-inch (23cm) springform pan. Use the back of a spoon or the bottom of a glass to compact the crust.
    - Refrigerate the crust while you prepare the filling.
2. **Make the cheesecake filling:**
    - In a large mixing bowl, combine the twaróg (or farmer's cheese) and cream cheese. Use a hand mixer or stand mixer fitted with the paddle attachment to beat until smooth and creamy.
    - Add the powdered sugar, lemon zest, lemon juice, and vanilla extract. Beat until well combined and smooth.
    - In a separate bowl, whip the heavy cream until stiff peaks form.
    - Gently fold the whipped cream into the cheese mixture until evenly incorporated and smooth.
3. **Assemble the cheesecake:**
    - Remove the prepared crust from the refrigerator.
    - Pour the cheesecake filling over the crust, spreading it evenly with a spatula.
4. **Chill the cheesecake:**
    - Cover the cheesecake with plastic wrap and refrigerate for at least 4 hours, or preferably overnight, to allow it to set and firm up.
5. **Serve:**
    - Before serving, run a knife around the edges of the springform pan to loosen the cheesecake. Release the sides of the pan and transfer the cheesecake to a serving platter.

- Garnish the top with fresh berries, fruit compote, or fruit preserves if desired.
6. **Enjoy your Sernik na zimno (Cold cheesecake)!**

This chilled cheesecake is creamy, light, and tangy with a hint of lemon. It's a delightful dessert that's perfect for warm weather or any occasion where you want to enjoy a refreshing treat.

Miodownik (Honey cake)

Ingredients:

For the cake layers:

- 4 cups (500g) all-purpose flour

- 1 cup (200g) granulated sugar
- 4 large eggs
- 1 cup (240ml) honey
- 1 cup (240ml) vegetable oil
- 1 teaspoon baking soda
- 1 teaspoon ground cinnamon
- 1/2 teaspoon ground cloves
- 1/2 teaspoon ground nutmeg
- Zest of 1 lemon
- Zest of 1 orange
- 1/2 cup (120ml) strong brewed coffee, cooled

For the frosting:

- 2 cups (480ml) heavy cream
- 1/2 cup (100g) granulated sugar
- 16 oz (450g) mascarpone cheese or cream cheese, softened
- 1 teaspoon vanilla extract

Optional garnish:

- Chopped nuts (such as walnuts or almonds)
- Cocoa powder or chocolate shavings

Instructions:

1. **Prepare the cake layers:**
    - Preheat your oven to 350°F (180°C). Grease and flour two 9-inch (23cm) round cake pans.
    - In a large mixing bowl, whisk together the flour, sugar, baking soda, cinnamon, cloves, and nutmeg.
    - In another bowl, beat the eggs with an electric mixer until frothy. Add the honey, vegetable oil, lemon zest, orange zest, and brewed coffee. Mix until well combined.
    - Gradually add the wet ingredients to the dry ingredients, mixing until smooth and well incorporated.
    - Divide the batter evenly between the prepared cake pans.
    - Bake in the preheated oven for 25-30 minutes, or until a toothpick inserted into the center comes out clean.
    - Remove from the oven and let the cakes cool in the pans for 10 minutes, then transfer them to a wire rack to cool completely.
2. **Make the frosting:**
    - In a chilled mixing bowl, whip the heavy cream with the granulated sugar until stiff peaks form.

- In another bowl, beat the mascarpone cheese or cream cheese until smooth and creamy. Add the vanilla extract and mix until combined.
- Gently fold the whipped cream into the mascarpone cheese until smooth and fluffy. Be careful not to overmix.

3. **Assemble the cake:**
    - Place one cake layer on a serving plate or cake stand.
    - Spread a generous amount of the frosting over the top of the cake layer, smoothing it out evenly with a spatula.
    - Place the second cake layer on top and spread the remaining frosting over the top and sides of the cake. Use a spatula to create swirls or peaks for decoration.
4. **Garnish (optional):**
    - Sprinkle chopped nuts over the top of the cake, or dust with cocoa powder or chocolate shavings for added decoration.
5. **Chill and serve:**
    - Refrigerate the cake for at least 2 hours before serving to allow the flavors to meld and the frosting to set.
6. **Enjoy your Miodownik (Honey cake)!**

This moist and flavorful Polish dessert is perfect for special occasions or as a delightful treat with a cup of coffee or tea. The combination of honey, spices, and creamy frosting makes it a true delight for dessert lovers.

Kremowka papieska (Papal cream cake)

Ingredients:

For the puff pastry:

- 2 sheets of store-bought puff pastry (about 9x9 inches each), thawed if frozen

For the custard filling:

- 2 cups (480ml) whole milk
- 1/2 cup (100g) granulated sugar
- 1/4 cup (30g) cornstarch
- 4 large egg yolks
- 1 teaspoon vanilla extract
- 1 cup (240ml) heavy cream, chilled
- 2 tablespoons powdered sugar (optional, for dusting)

Instructions:

1. **Prepare the puff pastry:**
   - Preheat your oven to 400°F (200°C). Line a baking sheet with parchment paper.
   - Place one sheet of puff pastry on the prepared baking sheet. Prick the pastry all over with a fork to prevent it from puffing up too much during baking.
   - Bake the puff pastry sheet in the preheated oven for 15-18 minutes, or until golden brown and puffed up. Repeat with the second sheet of puff pastry. Let them cool completely on a wire rack.
2. **Make the custard filling:**
   - In a medium saucepan, heat the milk over medium heat until it just begins to simmer. Remove from heat.
   - In a mixing bowl, whisk together the sugar, cornstarch, and egg yolks until smooth and creamy.
   - Gradually pour the hot milk into the egg yolk mixture, whisking constantly to temper the eggs.
   - Return the mixture to the saucepan and cook over medium heat, stirring constantly, until thickened and the mixture coats the back of a spoon (about 5-7 minutes).
   - Remove from heat and stir in the vanilla extract. Transfer the custard to a bowl and cover with plastic wrap directly on the surface to prevent a skin from forming. Let it cool to room temperature, then refrigerate until chilled.
3. **Assemble the Kremówka Papieska:**
   - Once the puff pastry sheets and custard filling are completely cooled, place one sheet of puff pastry on a serving platter or cake stand.
   - Spread the chilled custard filling evenly over the puff pastry sheet.
   - Place the second sheet of puff pastry on top of the custard filling.
4. **Chill and serve:**
   - Refrigerate the Kremówka Papieska for at least 2 hours, or until the custard filling is set.
5. **Optional garnish:**
   - Before serving, dust the top with powdered sugar for decoration.
6. **Enjoy your Kremówka Papieska (Papal Cream Cake)!**

This delightful Polish dessert is creamy, light, and perfect for any occasion. It's a wonderful homage to Pope John Paul II's love for this traditional treat from his homeland.

Makowiec (Poppy seed roll)

Ingredients:

For the dough:

- 4 cups (500g) all-purpose flour

- 1/2 cup (100g) granulated sugar
- 1/2 teaspoon salt
- 1/2 cup (120ml) warm milk
- 1/2 cup (120ml) warm water
- 2 1/4 teaspoons (1 packet) active dry yeast
- 2 large eggs, beaten
- 1/2 cup (115g) unsalted butter, melted and cooled

For the poppy seed filling:

- 1 1/2 cups (225g) ground poppy seeds
- 1 cup (240ml) milk
- 1/2 cup (100g) granulated sugar
- 1/2 cup (115g) unsalted butter
- 1/2 cup (75g) raisins (optional)
- 1/2 cup (75g) chopped nuts (such as walnuts or almonds)
- 1/4 cup (60ml) honey
- Zest of 1 lemon
- Zest of 1 orange
- 1 teaspoon vanilla extract

For brushing:

- 1 egg yolk mixed with 1 tablespoon milk, for egg wash

For garnish (optional):

- Powdered sugar, for dusting

Instructions:

1. **Prepare the dough:**
   - In a small bowl, dissolve the yeast and a pinch of sugar in warm water. Let it sit for 5-10 minutes until frothy.
   - In a large mixing bowl, combine the flour, sugar, and salt. Make a well in the center and add the warm milk, beaten eggs, melted butter, and the yeast mixture.
   - Mix the ingredients together until a soft dough forms.
   - Turn the dough out onto a floured surface and knead for about 8-10 minutes, or until smooth and elastic. Alternatively, you can use a stand mixer fitted with a dough hook for kneading.
   - Place the dough in a greased bowl, cover with a clean kitchen towel or plastic wrap, and let it rise in a warm place for about 1-2 hours, or until doubled in size.
2. **Make the poppy seed filling:**
   - In a saucepan, combine the ground poppy seeds, milk, sugar, butter, raisins (if using), and chopped nuts.

- Cook over medium heat, stirring constantly, until the mixture thickens and comes together (about 10-15 minutes).
- Remove from heat and stir in the honey, lemon zest, orange zest, and vanilla extract. Let the filling cool completely.

3. **Assemble the Makowiec:**
   - Punch down the risen dough and roll it out on a lightly floured surface into a rectangle about 12x16 inches (30x40cm).
   - Spread the cooled poppy seed filling evenly over the dough, leaving a small border around the edges.
   - Starting from one long edge, tightly roll up the dough into a log shape.
   - Place the rolled dough seam side down on a parchment-lined baking sheet, shaping it into a crescent or oval shape.
4. **Second rise:**
   - Cover the Makowiec loosely with a clean kitchen towel and let it rise in a warm place for another 30-45 minutes, or until slightly puffed.
5. **Bake:**
   - Preheat your oven to 350°F (180°C).
   - Brush the top of the Makowiec with the egg yolk and milk mixture.
   - Bake in the preheated oven for 30-35 minutes, or until golden brown and cooked through. If the top begins to brown too quickly, cover loosely with foil.
6. **Cool and garnish:**
   - Remove the Makowiec from the oven and let it cool on a wire rack.
   - Once cooled, dust with powdered sugar for decoration, if desired.
7. **Slice and serve:**
   - Slice the Makowiec into pieces and serve at room temperature.
8. **Enjoy your Makowiec (Poppy seed roll)!**

This delicious Polish dessert is best enjoyed with a cup of coffee or tea. It's rich with poppy seed flavor and has a delightful sweetness from the filling. Makowiec is a wonderful treat to share with family and friends during festive occasions or any time you crave a special homemade dessert.